Managing People

Managing People

Rosemary Thomson

*Published in association with
the Institute of Management*

Butterworth-Heinemann Ltd
Linacre House, Jordan Hill, Oxford OX2 8DP

℟ A member of the Reed Elsevier plc group

OXFORD   LONDON   BOSTON
MUNICH   NEW DELHI   SINGAPORE   SYDNEY
TOKYO   TORONTO   WELLINGTON

First published 1993
Reprinted 1993, 1994, 1995

British Library Cataloguing in Publication Data
Thomson, Rosemary
  Managing People
  I. Title
  658.3

ISBN 0 7506 0666 5

Printed and bound in Great Britain by Clays Ltd, St Ives plc

Contents

Series adviser's preface

This book is one of a series designed for people wanting to develop their capabilities as managers. You might think that there isn't anything very new in that. In one way you would be right. The fact that very many people want to learn to become better managers is not new, and for many years a wide range of approaches to such learning and development has been available. These have included courses leading to formal qualifications, organizationally-based management development programmes and a whole variety of self-study materials. A copious literature, extending from academic textbooks to sometimes idiosyncratic prescriptions from successful managers and consultants, has existed to aid – or perhaps confuse the potential seeker after managerial truth and enlightenment.

So what is new about this series? In fact, a great deal – marking in some ways a revolution in our thinking both about the art of managing and also the process of developing managers.

Where did it all begin? Like most revolutions, although there may be a single, identifiable act that precipitated the uprising, the roots of discontent are many and long-established. The debate about the performance of British managers, the way managers are educated and trained, and the extent to which shortcomings in both these areas have contributed to our economic decline, has been running for several decades.

Until recently, this debate had been marked by periods of frenetic activity-stimulated by some report or enquiry and perhaps ending in some new initiatives or policy changes – followed by relatively long periods of comparative calm. But the underlying causes for concern persisted. Basically, the majority of managers in the UK appeared to have little or no training for their role, certainly far less than their counterparts in our major competitor nations. And there was concern about the nature, style and appropriateness of the management education and training that was available.

The catalyst for this latest revolution came in late 1986 and early 1987, when three major reports reopened the whole issue. The 1987 reports were *The Making of British Managers* by John Constable and Roger McCormick, carried out for the British Institute of Management and the CBI, and *The Making of Managers* by Charles Handy, carried out for the (then) Manpower Services Commission, National Economic Development Office and British Institute of Management. The 1986 report, which often receives less recognition than it deserves as a key contribution to the recent changes, was *Management Training: context and process* by Iain Mangham and Mick Silver, carried out for the Economic and Social Research Council and the Department of Trade and Industry.

It is not the place to review in detail what the reports said. Indeed, they and their consequences are discussed in several places in this series of books. But essentially they confirmed that:

- British managers were undertrained by comparison with their counterparts internationally.
- The majority of employers invested far too little in training and developing their managers.
- Many employers found it difficult to specify with any degree of detail just what it was that they required successful managers to be able to do.

The Constable/McCormick and Handy reports advanced various recommendations for addressing these problems, involving an expansion of management education and development, a reformed structure of qualifications and a commitment from employers to a code of practice for management development. While this analysis was not new, and had echoes of much that had been said in earlier debates, this time a few leading individuals determined that the response should be both radical and permanent. The response was coordinated by the newly-established Council for Management Education and Development (now the National Forum for Management Education and Development (NFMED)) under the energetic and visionary leadership of Bob (now Sir Bob) Reid of Shell UK (now chairman of the British Railways Board).

Under the umbrella of NFMED a series of employer-led working parties tackled the problem of defining what it was that managers should be able to do, and how this differed for people at different levels in their organizations; how this satisfactory ability to perform might be verified; and how an appropriate structure of management qualifications could be put in place. This work drew upon the methods used to specify vocational standards in industry and commerce, and led to the development and introduction of competence-based management standards and qualifications. In this context, competence is defined as the ability to perform the activities within an occupation or function to the standards expected in employment.

It is this competence-based approach that is new in our thinking about the manager's capabilities. It is also what is new about this series of books, in that they are designed to support both this new structure of management standards, and of development activities based on it. The series was originally commissioned to support the Institute of Management's Certificate and Diploma qualifications, which were one of the first to be based on the new standards. However, these books are equally appropriate to any university, college or indeed company course leading to a certificate in management or diploma in management studies.

The standards were specified through an extensive process of consultation with a large number of managers in organizations of many different types and sizes. They are therefore employment based and employer-supported. And they fill the gap that Mangham and Silver identified − now we do have a language to describe what it is employers want their managers to be able to do − at least in part.

If you are engaged in any form of management development leading to a certificate or diploma qualification conforming to the national management standards, then you are probably already familiar with most of the key ideas on which the standards are based. To achieve their key purpose, which is defined as achieving the organization's objectives and continuously improving its performance, managers need to perform four key roles: managing operations, managing finance, managing people and managing information. Each of these key roles has a sub-structure of units and elements, each with associated performance and assessment criteria.

The reason for the qualification 'in part' is that organizations are different, and jobs within them are different. Thus the generic management standards probably do not cover all the management competences that you may need to possess in your job. There are almost certainly additional things, specific to your own situation in your own organization, that you need to be able to do. The standards are necessary, but almost certainly not sufficient. Only you, in discussion with your boss, will be able to decide what other capabilities you need to possess. But the standards are a place to start, a basis on which to build. Once you have demonstrated your proficiency against the standards, it will stand you in good stead as you progress through your organization, or change jobs.

So how do the new standards change the process by which you develop yourself as a manager? They change the process of development, or of gaining a management qualification, quite a lot. It is no longer a question of acquiring information and facts, perhaps by being 'taught' in some classroom environment, and then being tested to see what you can recall. It involves demonstrating, in a quite specific way, that you can do certain things to a particular standard of performance. And because of this, it puts a much greater onus on you to manage your own development, to decide how you can demonstrate any particular competence, what evidence you need to present, and how you can collect it. Of course, there will always be people to advise and guide you in this, if you need help.

But there is another dimension, and it is to this that this series of books is addressed. While the standards stress ability to perform, they do not ignore the traditional knowledge base that has been associated with management studies . Rather, they set this in a different context. The standards are supported by 'underpinning knowledge and understanding' which has three components:

- Purpose and context, which is knowledge and understanding of the manager's objectives, and of the relevant organizational and environmental influences, opportunities and values.
- Principles and methods, which is knowledge and understanding of the theories, models, principles, methods and techniques that provide the basis of competent managerial performance.
- Data, which is knowledge and understanding of specific facts likely to be important to meeting the standards.

Possession of the relevant knowledge and understanding underpinning the standards is needed to support competent managerial performance as specified in the standards. It also has an important role in supporting the transferability of management capabilities. It helps to ensure that you have done more than learned 'the way we do things around here' in your own organization. It indicates a recognition of the wider things which underpin competence, and that you will be able to change jobs or organizations and still be able to perform effectively.

These books cover the knowledge and understanding underpinning the management standards, most specifically in the category of principles and methods. But their coverage is not limited to the minimum required by the standards, and extends in both depth and breadth in many areas. The authors have tried to approach these underlying principles and methods in a practical way. They use many short cases and examples which we hope will demonstrate how, in practice, the principles and methods, and knowledge of purpose and context plus data, support the ability to perform as required by the management standards. In particular we hope that this type of presentation will enable you to identify and learn from similar examples in your own managerial work.

You will already have noticed that one consequence of this new focus on the standards is that the traditional 'functional' packages of knowledge and theory do not appear. The standard textbook titles such as 'quantitative methods', 'production management', 'organizational behaviour' etc. disappear. Instead, principles and methods have been collected together in clusters that more closely match the key roles within the standards. You will also find a small degree of overlap in some of the volumes, because some principles and methods support several of the individual units within the standards. We hope you will find this useful reinforcement.

Having described the positive aspects of standards-based management development, it would be wrong to finish without a few cautionary remarks. The developments described above may seem simple, logical and uncontroversial. It did not always seem that way in the years of work which led up to the introduction of the standards. To revert to the revolution analogy, the process has been marked by ideological conflict and battles over sovereignty and territory. It has sometimes been unclear which side various parties are on − and indeed how many sides there are! The revolution, if well advanced, is not at an end. Guerrilla warfare continues in parts of the territory.

Perhaps the best way of describing this is to say that, while competence-based standards are widely recognized as at least a major part of the answer to improving managerial performance, they are not the whole answer. There is still some debate about the way competences are defined, and whether those in the standards are the most appropriate on which to base assessment of managerial performance. There are other models of management competences than those in the standards.

There is also a danger in separating management performance into a set of discrete components. The whole is, and needs to be, more than the sum of the parts. Just like bowling an off-break in cricket, practising a golf swing or forehand drive in tennis, you have to combine all the separate movements into a smooth, flowing action. How you combine the competences, and build on them, will mark your own individual style as a manager.

We should also be careful not to see the standards as set in stone. They determine what today's managers need to be able to do. As the arena in which managers operate changes, then so will the standards. The lesson for all of us as managers is that we need to go on learning and developing, acquiring new skills or refining existing ones. Obtaining your certificate or diploma is like passing a mile post, not crossing the finishing line.

All the changes and developments of recent years have brought management qualifications, and the processes by which they are gained, much closer to your job as a manager. We hope these books support this process by providing bridges between your own experience and the underlying principles and methods which will help you to demonstrate your competence. Already, there is a lot of evidence that managers enjoy the challenge of demonstrating competence, and find immediate benefits in their jobs from the programmes based on these new-style qualifications. We hope you do too. Good luck in your career development.

Paul Jervis

Acknowledgements

The author acknowledges ideas and concepts contained in Open University, Open Business School courses, in particular 'The Effective Manager'.

Several of the examples of both good and bad practice in this book have been reported in *Personnel Management*, the journal of the Institute of Personnel Management and published by Personnel Publications Ltd. Where appropriate, the legal and regulatory frameworks surrounding the management of people have been checked with *The Personnel Manager's Factbook* (Gee), which is updated regularly.

1 Managing people in the twenty-first century

Introduction

In this chapter, we are going to take an overview of what a manager needs to do in relation to managing people in a changing environment. We will be looking at:

- The role of management research.
- Your job as a manager.
- National developments in management training.
- Trends in the 1990s and beyond.
- How to use this book.

Management in practice

It may seem strange to start a section on 'management in practice' by looking at the role of management research, but without such research we would have very little real idea of what managers do and how they do it. The kind of research we will be using in this book has been carried out mainly on practising managers and, as such, is rooted in reality.

Most management research involves the painstaking study of working managers over a period of time before drawing conclusions from what the researcher has observed or investigated. These conclusions can be used to define the main elements of a manager's job and to predict how his or her performance of that job may be improved. Obviously, it is generalized since, as you will see in Chapter 4, managers and the people they manage all come from different backgrounds, have differing degrees of knowledge and experience and behave in different ways. However, management research seeks to give us explanations of why people behave as they do and how that behaviour can be changed if necessary.

In this book, we will only be touching on a few areas of significant research in management; some of this research will have been around for a long time, but that does not make it any less important for today's managers. Some of it will be very recent, reflecting the changing activities and attitudes of organizations and their managers.

What does a manager do?

At the end of this chapter, you will be asked to undertake a diary exercise to try to define what you do in your job as a manager. Listing your key responsibilities as they may be defined in your job description is one way — but how do you classify what you do on a day-to-day basis? What was the first managerial task you undertook this morning? Could you relate it clearly to one of your key responsibilities?

> Catherine works as a junior manager in the Banking Section of the Cashier's Department in a Regional Authority. She lists as her main responsibility the banking of all monies received in the Region. This involves supervising clerks who sort out cash, cheques and Giro pay-in slips by location and check these against control sheets. She is responsible for checking any discrepancies in the daily total and informing other departments responsible for errors. However, the first thing she did one morning was to confirm the holiday rota with her staff; on another morning, she had to spend some time training a new recruit to the Section and then attend a monthly meeting on staff appraisal in the Authority; on yet another morning, she had to talk to one of the clerks about persistent lateness ... and so on. None of these tasks closely related to her key responsibilities, yet they were all part of her job.

One way of looking at your role as a manager is to classify what you do into the elements of the job. Henri Fayol, a mining engineer by training, spent his working life in a French mining and metallurgical combine, first as an engineer and then moving into general management, finally becoming managing director. From his prolonged observation of managers, he concluded that every managerial job contained the same five elements, although individual managers in different industries might lay more stress on some elements than on others.

Fayol's five elements of management were:

- *Forecasting and planning* — looking to the future; ensuring the objectives of the organization are being met; short- and long-term forecasting; being able to adapt plans as a circumstances change; attempting to predict what is going to happen.
- *Organizing* — ensuring that the structure of the organization allows its basic activities to be carried out; giving direction; defining responsibilities; making decisions and backing these up by an efficient system for selecting and training staff.
- *Commanding* — we might prefer to use the word 'leading' here since this refers to the relationship between a manager and his or

her subordinates in relation to the task being performed including counselling, appraisal, giving feedback, allocating work and so on.
- *Coordinating* – ensuring that individuals, teams and departments work in harmony towards common organizational goals; keeping all activities in perspective with regard to the overall aims of the organization.
- *Controlling* – ensuring that the other four elements are being carried out; operating sanctions if necessary (Pugh and Hickson, 1989).

Catherine's early morning activities could readily have been classified into these elements. The holiday rota involved forecasting and planning as well as coordination; the training session required organizing as did the staff appraisal system; commanding and controlling were involved in her talk with the person who was not performing adequately.

Although Fayol undertook his research earlier this century and his book *Administration Industrielle et Generale* was first published in 1916, his framework for looking at what a manager does is still valid today.

National developments in management training

A much more recent exercise was undertaken in the UK at the end of the 1980s by the Management Charter Initiative. This national body used functional analysis of the work of a large number of British practising managers to define the 'competences' needed at junior and middle management levels. Competence involves not only vocational skills, but the knowledge and understanding which underpins them. A large number of organizations including British Telecom, Safeway, the National Health Service and Lucas have adopted this competence-based approach to management training and, indeed, in some organizations, linked it to recruitment, induction, staff appraisal and promotion. Work is proceeding to identify competences at levels above middle management, to develop standards for supervisors and to link up with European counterparts to devise international standards of competence.

This competence-based approach to management development arose as the result of two major reports published in 1987, 'The Making of Managers' (Handy et al) and 'The Making of British Managers' (Constable and McCormick). These reports showed how far behind its European and world counterparts the UK was in the extent of its training and development of managers. It is also related to the development of National Vocational Qualifications (NVQs) which are job-related qualifications, modelled on the assumption of specific active tasks which can be demonstrated and assessed in a work situation or simulation.

At the time of writing (1992), it would be fair to say that the competence-based approach has its addicts and its opponents. Of organizations surveyed in mid-1991, 70 per cent did not feel that this approach had had any influence on the way in which their managers were trained or developed. The survey, carried out by Price Waterhouse, concluded that there remained a lack of strategic-level commitment to management development − only 50 per cent of the companies involved had a formal, written policy covering the development of managers.

INVESTIGATE

- *Does your organization have a formal policy on management training and development?*
- *Does your organization adopt a competence-based approach to training?*
- *If your organization does not provide continuous management training and development, what local opportunities are open to you?*

Trends in the 1990s and beyond

In the 1990s, people are going to be even more crucial to the success or failure of organizations. Peter Herriot, Professor of Occupational Psychology at Birkbeck College, University of London, has indentified five trends which will be critical in determining whether organizations survive this last decade of the twentieth century (Herriot, 1989).

The quality imperative

The first of these is increased competition, not only from our European counterparts but from other parts of the world as well. Herriot argues that quality of goods and services will be the criterion for competitive advantage, so the organization which makes quality a top priority is more likely to succeed. Many organizations are now conforming to the quality standards set by the British Standards Institute (BS 5750) and to more specific industry- or sector-related standards as well as the international quality standards (ISO 9000). Meeting these standards, however, is only the baseline for quality and should be seen as a springboard for further initiatives such as the Royal Mail 'Customer first' programme, British Airways' programme on customer care, and the Inland Revenue which set itself new quality standards in 1992.

The information technology imperative

A second trend is the impact of information technology, particularly in the area of providing informational support for decision-making. The growth of on-line data, accessible to everyone in the organization, will improve the quality and speed of decision-making at all levels which will have an effect on traditional staffing levels. As everyone has access to essential information, people in organizations gain more power and take on greater responsibility. This has an effect on the hierarchical structure of the organization and on the types of people it recruits and on their development and retention.

The evolutionary imperative

The third trend is the catalytic effect of the increasing number of mergers and take-overs. Small and medium-sized organizations tend to merge or be taken over in the interests of corporate survival. As these conglomerates acquire more businesses, they tend to decentralize and create new divisions, producing different goods and services, requiring diverse and new skills and competences in the people who work in them.

The communication imperative

Fourth, and this is linked to the growth in information technology, the knowledge of the organization's external environment is much more accessible than ever before. For example, there is instant access to world money markets through on-line data; communication is fast and efficient by electronic means; worldwide media coverage provides us with knowledge of events as they take place. This enables organizations, and people, to be more responsive to changes in national and international contexts.

The imperative of change

With the external environment constantly changing, however, bureaucratic organizations are not able to respond quickly enough. So, in order to survive and succeed, organizations will need to move away from highly structured spans of control, long lead-in times and endless discussions in committees to a more responsive structure which may involve redundancies and streamlining (Herriot, 1989).

IBM (UK), which operates in the fast-changing industry of information technology, needed to change its ratio of support workers to employees directly earning revenue as a result of price cuts

> by competitors, particularly in the personal computer market. In 1989, 55 per cent of all IBM (UK) employees were in the non-manufacturing, support area of the business and this had to be reduced to 35 per cent, while increasing the number of direct-revenue earning employees. A large number of senior professionals and managers took early retirement or a redundancy package, resulting in a reorganization of the company's structure.

The implications of these trends are important for managers, particularly in the management of people. It is more essential than ever before — and part of the manager's role in forecasting and planning — to recruit, develop and keep the right people.

How to use this book

This book has been written to give managers the essential knowledge and understanding which will underpin their competence in management in practice. This involves knowledge of some of the more important research in the area and of recent developments, but it also involves recognition of what is 'good practice' in the management of people. Examples of practice, good and bad, are given throughout in the boxed sections within each chapter; this information is in the public domain and can be found in any newspaper or professional journal.

The contents list will give you an idea of the coverage of the subject area, so you can use the book as a reference when you want to find out more about a particular idea or set of skills. Or you can read it through from beginning to end since it is not designed to be an 'academic' text. It covers the areas of knowledge and understanding which underpin the units of competence developed by the Management Charter Initiative in their Management Standards at Levels I and II, so you can also use the book to help you gain a qualification in management.

Each chapter consists of an introduction, setting the scene for what is to come. The main section, 'Management in practice', covers research, ideas and practical examples of the subject area. It also contains a number of points where you are asked to stop reading and think about how the ideas relate to practice in your own organization. These points are indicated by the word 'INVESTIGATE', since they are designed to involve you in finding out about how or why things happen in your workplace. Where appropriate, some guidelines about relevant legal and regulatory frameworks are included.

At the end of each chapter there is a summary of the main content and some activities which you might like to try out to check your understanding of what you have read or how you might apply some of the ideas in your own job. Finally, each chapter lists some books on the subject which you might like to read if you want to find out more about a particular aspect of managing people.

Summary

This chapter has introduced you to what managers do in their everyday jobs and how they will need to take account of a number of trends in the 1990s and beyond. They will also need to be trained to meet the challenges and opportunities of managing in the twenty-first century if their organizations are to succeed.

Activities

1   *Your role as a manager*   Over the next few days, try to keep a 'diary' of what you actually do in your job. You might find it useful to use the headings devised by Fayol for classifying the elements of management. You might need to keep a 'miscellaneous' heading for those tasks which do not immediately fall into Fayol's classification.

2   *Trends for the 1990s and beyond*   Can you identify any changes that have taken place in your organization over the past few years which are a response to the trends identified by Peter Herriot? Can you foresee any changes that your organization may have to undertake in the future in order to respond to these trends more effectively?

References

Constable, J. and McCormick, R. (1987) *The Making of British Managers*, Report for the British Institute of Management and the Confederation of British Industry. (Available from BIM, Corby, Northants)

Fayol, H. (1949 [1916]) *General and Industrial Management* (trans. Storrs), Pitman, London

Handy, C., Gow, I., Gordon, C., Randlesome, C. and Moloney, M. (1987) *The Making of Managers*, National Economic Development Office, London

Herriot, P. (1989) *Recruitment in the 90s*, Institute of Personnel Management, London

Pugh, D. S. and Hickson, D. J. (1989) *Writers on Organizations*, Penguin Business Books, Harmondsworth

Further reading

Boyatzis, R. R. (1982) *The Competent Manager: a Model for Effective Performance*, John Wiley, New York

Easterby-Smith, M. (1986) *Evaluation of Management Education, Training and Development*, Gower, London

Silver, M. (1991) *Competent to Manage: Approaches to Management Training and Development*, Routledge, London

2 Recruiting the right people

Introduction

This chapter is concerned with defining future staff requirements and determining the specifications necessary to recruit quality people, particularly in your own area of responsibility although these should, ideally, be set in a context of overall organizational personnel requirements. To do this, you need to be able to:

1 Identify, define and assess the competences of the people who are currently working in your organization, department or team depending on your level of managerial responsibility.
2 Analyse the content of the current jobs under your control.
3 Draw up detailed job descriptions for each one.
4 Determine future competence requirements in relation to current and future work demands and job roles.
5 For new jobs or for vacancies in existing work, draw up an employee specification, taking into account the role of that job in your team and organizational structure.
6 Consider the financial position of your area of responsibility relating to salary/wage costs.
7 Inform and consult with other people in the organization about your recruitment problems and proposals and encourage them to offer their ideas and views.

Management in practice

The trends for the 1990s which were identified in Chapter 1 have considerable implications for the staff we recruit. According to Peter Herriot (1989), organizations will need:

- more engineers, scientists and computer people;
- more professionals;
- more managers;
- more technicians;
- more designers, marketers and salespeople.

There will be a need for people who can operate in the rest of Europe; for managers familiar with the use of information technology; for people who understand the environment in which the organization operates; for people who are willing and able to acquire new skills and knowledge; for people able to make decisions as the context and environment change. Organizations and their managers will need to be involved in human resource auditing and planning to determine their future needs.

Planning for the future is no longer easy as the future becomes less and less predictable. You can no longer afford to recruit staff on job descriptions that have been around for years; you are going to need people who can be adaptable and respond to new challenges. This means, too, that you should look beyond your normal sources of staff since these may no longer be appropriate for your needs.

You will also need to be aware of current and new legislation governing the recruitment of people in a wider European labour market; in particular, you need to avoid discrimination on the grounds of gender, race or disability.

Determining human resource requirements

Human resource planning has been around for more than a quarter of a century. Initially, it was based on complex mathematical models which were incomprehensible to anyone but mathematicians. These models were intended to forecast long-term trends but they failed to operate successfully in attempts to reduce unemployment or to anticipate skill shortages. The pace of change outran the adequacy of this means of planning for the future.

During the 1970s, human resource accounting became popular, i.e. applying principles of financial accounting to human resources. However, human resources, unlike fixed assets, tend to appreciate with experience rather than depreciate with age and this appreciation is very difficult to estimate in financial terms (Pearson, 1991). In the mid-1980s, scenario planning came into favour. This involved the design of models of best and worst scenarios as far as organizational human resource needs were concerned and could be computerized to produce 'what if' scenarios. What if ... there is a major UK or European recession? What if ... new technology overtakes the skills of current staff? It is possible, given the reluctance of organizations to change, that your own organization uses one or other of these methods despite their failure to predict human resource needs with any accuracy.

INVESTIGATE

- *What methods does your organization use to plan for future staffing levels?*

Current thinking suggests that an organizational strategy which links recruitment with development and retention of its staff has more chance of success, providing the trends identified in Chapter 1 are taken into account. This involves line managers rather than leaving everything to the personnel specialists and involves four stages:

1 Categorization – the arrangement of people into job-related groups such as sales assistants, nurses, machine operators and so on, while recognizing that any simple category is only provisional and liable to change.
2 Enumeration – which includes a number of quantitative measures relevant to the organization; some of these can be derived from staff record systems; others may require surveys of staff to be carried out.
3 Description – presentation of the data gained from categorization and enumeration.
4 Explanation – explaining the implications of the data to management and other people.

The material gathered from conducting an audit of existing staff in this way can be used to create a Human Resource Plan with provisions for recruitment, training, transfers, promotion and outplacement (Pearson, 1991).

The first stage in the recruitment process is to determine human resource needs now and in the future. Any strategic plan for the future of an organization needs to be expressed not only in terms of what the organization expects to achieve, but also the ways in which these achievements can be fulfilled. This includes the numbers and type of staff the organization is likely to need in both the short-term and long-term future.

If your organization has a well drawn-up strategic plan or a clear mission statement, these should be your first sources of information about human resource needs. The plan, ideally, should identify the number of jobs which will exist if the organization is to achieve its objectives and the types of skills and knowledge jobholders will require. If no strategic plan exists, you may have to draw one up for your own department or area of responsibility. To do this, you need to have a clear idea of your objectives over the period covered by your planning – this may be over three, four, five or more years – and be able to state them in unambiguous terms so that other people can understand them. You then need to 'operationalize' these objectives by stating how they can be achieved and what resources, particularly in relation to people and skills, will be required to make these achievements possible. This is obviously an area in which you will need the help and expertise of other people in your organization.

INVESTIGATE

• *Find a copy of your organization's strategic plan or mission statement. Does it give a clear indication of the type and numbers of staff the organization will need in the future?*

Job analysis: auditing existing human resources

The first stage in developing a plan for the future involves analysing the skills and knowledge already available to you amongst the people already working for you — sometimes called a Human Resource Audit. In this way, you can begin to identify skill deficiencies and plan to remedy these deficiencies through recruitment.

Recruiting staff for a job which already exists needs to take into account ways in which that job may change in the future. But are you sure that you know what the job entails at the moment? Looking at an existing job description may be misleading since it is likely, if the jobholder has been in the job for some time, that the job has already changed within that period.

Let us assume that a member of your staff has handed in his/her notice and you have a vacancy to fill. How do you find out what the job really entails? We have already said that existing job descriptions can be unreliable; so, too, can be the description of the job by the present jobholder. Try analysing your own job and see how difficult it is. The jobholder's description is only of value if it is supported by other evidence. You can use any combination of the following methods for analysing jobs:

• Question the present jobholder about the job using a written questionnaire.
• Give the present jobholder a list of possible tasks and ask him/her to select those that apply to this job.
• Interview the jobholder.
• Watch the jobholder performing the job.
• Ask other people what they think the job entails.
• Ask the jobholder to keep a diary of everything he/she does in performing the job.
• Do the job yourself for a few days and keep a detailed record.
• Involve the jobholder and his/her supervisor in determining which tasks contribute positively to satisfactory completion of the job and those which inhibit satisfactory job completion (critical incident technique).

Your objectives in carrying out this exercise are fourfold.

First, what is the purpose of the job? Is it necessary? Is it fulfilling its purpose?

Second, could the job be combined with other jobs to make it more fulfilling or could some parts of it be reallocated to make better use of the skills of other people in the department?

Third, could a full-time job be shared between two people working part-time? Could all or part of the job be carried out in the jobholder's home? Could more flexible working hours be introduced? This would enable you to widen your recruitment to include people who, for a variety of reasons, could not undertake either a full-time job or travel to and from home.

A number of companies are taking positive action to recruit and retain working mothers. Sainsbury, Boots and B&Q offer jobs where working hours are confined to school terms. ICI have improved their maternity pay and designed working hours which fit in with school hours and holidays; as a result, the number of women managers working for the company has increased. BHS has also adopted a system of flexible working hours. They offer two types of contract, one related to working during school terms only and another for employees who want to specify their own hours and are prepared to work on a standby basis.

INVESTIGATE

- *Does your organization operate any jobshare schemes or flexitime working? If not, could these be introduced?*

Fourth, what have I learned about the job from analysing it?

When you have gone through these processes, and you are satisfied that you have enough information about the job, and that this information is clear and unambiguous, you are almost ready to move on to write, or rewrite, a job description. But, bearing in mind the trends identified for the 1990s, you also need to consider whether the job as you have analysed it is likely to stay the same or to change in the foreseeable future. Will the next jobholder require different skills if the job is to change or grow? For example, is your organization planning to move into markets outside the UK and are you likely to need people who can speak languages other than English or who are willing to be mobile?

Job descriptions

ACAS, the Advisory, Conciliation and Arbitration Service, suggests that a job description should be drawn up under the following headings.

1 The title of the job

Most jobs have a title such as Project Manager, Filing Clerk, Supervisor and so on. Remember what was said earlier about categorizing people; is the old job title still valid after your analysis or does it need to be changed to reflect the changed nature of the job? Examine the current job title critically; does it really describe the job? And does it imply any descriptive discrimination in terms of race, gender or disability, e.g. salesman?

2 The main purpose of the job

Your job analysis should have teased this out and you should aim to describe the purpose of the job in one sentence. For example:

Job Title
Administrative Secretary
Main purpose of the job
Supervising the work of secretarial and clerical staff in the department in order to provide high quality secretarial support to the senior management team.

3 The main tasks of the job

Here, again, the job analysis should have identified these but you need to make them as clear as possible. Use verbs such as 'writing . . .', 'filing . . .', 'designing . . .', 'planning . . .' etc. which actively describe what the job involves. Avoid vague terms such as 'in charge of . . .'.

4 The scope of the job

You have already stated the main tasks of the job but this gives little indication of how important the job is. In this section you need to give an idea of, for example, the number of people for whom the jobholder would be responsible or the budget he/she would control or the value of the equipment or materials handled, and how the job itself relates to the overall work of the department or organization.

Employee specification – also known as person specification

Once you have completed a satisfactory job description, you should draw up a description of the type of person you feel would best perform the job. This should be done under four main headings and each heading should be subdivided into 'essential' and 'desirable' qualities in the person you are seeking. Those qualities which are categorized as 'essential' are necessary to adequate performance of the job; without them, the job could not be performed either effectively or efficiently. 'Desirable' qualities should be seen as additional assets which would enhance effective performance of the job.

Skills

These are what the jobholder should possess, or be capable of acquiring through experience or training in order to perform the job effectively. Your job analysis and job description should have identified these for you and you should include any skills which might be necessary for performance of the job if and when it changes in the future. Some manual skill requirements could be seen to discriminate against disabled people; in fact, the Disablement Advisory Service can provide equipment which can enable disabled people to perform most jobs.

> The voluntary organization, Action for Blind People has launched a new awareness programme to encourage employers to increase the number of visually impaired people in work. The programme aims to dispel some of the myths about the employment of blind or partially-sighted people since many employers believe that it will cost them more to provide equipment or that they are likely to be absent from the workplace more often than sighted employees. For this purpose, Action for Blind People provides an employer information pack, backed up by other services which they provide on a voluntary basis.

> Employers who take on staff with disabilities may be eligible for help under a number of schemes such as adaptation of premises or equipment grants although many people with disabilities can work with little or no special equipment. The Disabled Graduates Careers Information Service also offers advice to employers on preparing for applications, interviews and tests involving people with disabilities.

Knowledge

This may be technical, professional, administrative or organizational but it must be relevant to the effective performance of the job. Some highly specialized knowledge may be gained through provision for training in the job rather than be expected in applicants.

Experience

The amount of relevant experience, and the level, should be carefully assessed in relation to the requirements of the job itself. Some specifications discriminate unfairly against some groups of people. For example, if you felt current experience was essential, this would discriminate against women returners; you should ask yourself if this was not, in fact, a 'desirable' quality or, indeed, really necessary at all.

Attitudes

This subheading refers to behavioural qualities such as the ability to work in a team or to take initiative or work without supervision. Often, this is the hardest area of the employee specification against which to measure applicants and your selection procedure will need to be designed to determine whether or not candidates actually have the attitudes you consider important.

Everything you include in the employee specification should relate closely to your job description and should be capable of being measured so that you are able to make an informed and accurate decision about the best candidate for the job.

Methods of recruiting candidates

First of all, you have to decide whether you need to recruit candidates from outside the organization to take over a vacant job. If you have carried out an audit of the people in your area of responsibility, you should have a good idea of the skills, knowledge, experience and attitudes of your existing staff and it may make more sense to promote someone internally or to move someone sideways. You may also like to consider internal recruitment from other parts of your own organization.

Traditional sources of recruitment have usually been schools and further and higher education institutions, depending on your resource requirements. However, not only may these traditional sources fail to provide organizations with the quality of candidate they are looking for in the 1990s, there are less people available in this age group due to the decline in the birth rate. More and more organizations are turning away from the Oxbridge graduate trainee intake, finding that young people from the newer universities are better fitted for working in, for example, technical areas. Other organizations are deliberately broadening their recruitment base to include people from minority groups in an aim to discourage discrimination.

> The BBC has introduced a text telephone service to encourage people with impaired hearing to apply for a wide range of jobs.

Organizations that operate equal opportunities policies ensure that recruitment advertisements are not just placed in traditional white, middle-class newspapers and journals but in media which are read by people from different ethnic and religious backgrounds; they also take positive action to encourage the employment of people from all minority groups.

> The Metropolitan Police has included a sentence in its equal opportunities policy stating that it does not discriminate on the grounds of sexual orientation; this is seen as sending a positive message to job-seekers who have previously been deterred from joining the police force for fear of prejudice against homosexuals.

The criteria for methods of recruitment are that they should be cost-effective and that there is no hint of discrimination on sex or race grounds. In this country, it is still permissible to discriminate on the grounds of age — for example, 'The candidate should be aged between 25 and 40 ...' — although this is illegal in the United States and will probably be outlawed in Europe in the near future.

Apart from internal advertising and direct recruiting from schools, colleges and universities — the 'milk round' — other methods include:

- Advertising in local, national and international press, in the specialist and professional press, on radio, TV, teletext and in cinemas.
- Recruiting from Jobcentres.
- Using external consultants or 'headhunters', professional and recruitment agencies.
- Maintaining an internal databank of unsuccessful applicants for similar jobs.
- Attending professionally run Recruitment Fairs.

INVESTIGATE

- *Which sources of recruits does your organization use? Should you be thinking about widening the recruitment net by investigating other sources?*

Job advertisements

By far the most common method of recruitment is through advertisements; it is also the method most fraught with misunderstanding, misinterpretation and potential lawbreaking.

There has been considerable research into how people react to advertisements for jobs, both published and unpublished (Schofield, 1992). The main findings relevant to this chapter are:

- that readers scanning recruitment pages in newspapers and journals spend, on average, just one and a half seconds on each advertisement;
- that heavy black borders around advertisements are a barrier to scanning and fewer people read the advertisement inside;
- that the most important factor people look for in a job is interesting work, followed by prospects of promotion, salary, security, personal involvement with the job and education/training opportunities;
- that, where an individual is actually named in an advertisement as the person to whom job applications should be sent, there is a significantly higher response than if only a job title or department is given.

As already pointed out, one of the criteria of recruitment is that it is cost-effective. Poor job advertisements waste time and money since they attract candidates who are unsuitable for the job; good advertisements are specifically designed to attract candidates who can and want to do the job effectively. A good job advertisement should be designed to gain

- Attention
- Interest
- Desire
- Action

from the person reading it. It is easy to remember these four points using the mnemonic AIDA.

The first important point is the look of the advertisement and its headline. Remember, your reader is only going to spend an average of one and a half seconds scanning an advertisement so, if you want to catch the reader's attention, the headline is critical. To be most effective in attracting attention, it should describe clearly the job or the skill sought, perhaps accompanied by an eye-catching illustration or phrase.

The main factors people look for when seeking jobs were outlined above. This is the information you want to put across in your advertisement. Potential candidates also want to know where the job is going to be located, what they will be doing, whether they have the appropriate skills and experience, what they will be paid and what benefits the organization offers. This is where your job description and employee specification are invaluable.

In Japan, the search for graduate recruits is so fierce that small firms are offering horses, cows, tailor-made suits and apartments as enticements.

INVESTIGATE

● *Try to get hold of a recruitment advertisement your organization has used recently. In light of what you have just read, does it come up to standard?*

Further information for candidates: an Information Pack

Potential employees will also want to know more about the job than can be put in an advertisement – usually referred to as 'further particulars'.

Example of a poorly worded advertisement:

'Further particulars may be obtained on application to the Personnel Officer to whom typewritten curriculum vitae (six copies) with the names and addresses of two referees should be sent by ...'

This may be organizational practice, but is it really necessary? It is certainly discouraging and it says something about an organization which might put good candidates off. A better, user-friendly alternative is:

'For an information pack, including details of how to apply, please telephone Mary Adams on ...'

You are going to need further information for job candidates which can be drawn from the job description and employee specification. It should also include information about the organization as a whole. The Information Pack should 'sell' your organization to potential candidates and should contain:

- essential and realistic details of the job, and its place in the organization;
- information about the organization such as an Annual Report (if there is one) and some indication of its size, achievements and future plans;
- information about the essential and desirable qualities required for the post, drawn from your employee specification;
- the name and telephone number of someone in the organization (in agreement with that person) whom candidates can contact if they want to ask questions about the job or find out more from someone 'on the ground';
- information about how the selection process will be carried out (see Chapter 3).

> The British Ceramic Confederation has produced a brochure designed to recruit young people into the industry. It gives an overview of the ceramics industry and the kinds of career opportunities it offers in areas such as production, sales and marketing. The brochure includes studies of young people who have entered the industry from a range of backgrounds and is accompanied by a video.

INVESTIGATE

- *Does your organization send out an Information Pack or comprehensive information to job applicants?*

Applications

You are also going to have to consider in what form you want applications to be made. Your organization may have a standard application form which was designed many years ago and is now unsuitable for its purpose − have a look at it and decide whether it meets your needs or whether it needs to be adapted or redesigned. Any application form should be designed to give the maximum information about the candidate which is *relevant* to the requirements of the job. This can include relevant educational, technical and/or professional qualifications essential for performance of the job, previous job history and relevant experience and any special requirements such as the ability to speak a particular language or the need to hold a current driving licence if these are necessary to the performance of the job. The application form should not require details of marital status or dependants, nationality or disabilities; it should use the term 'forename' and not 'Christian name' since the latter is inappropriate for applicants of Arab origin.

You may also ask for a Curriculum Vitae (CV) or a letter of application instead of, or in addition to, a completed application form: look at the requirements of the job and decide which form(s) of application would be most useful when it comes to making an initial selection.

Finally, you have to ensure that in no way does your advertisement contravene the law governing discrimination in recruitment advertising; it should not suggest that the job is open only to persons of one sex, race or particular marital status unless the job is classified as a GOQ (see section on the legal and regulatory framework at the end of this chapter). If it does, a complaint may be lodged with the Equal Opportunities Commission or the Commission for Racial Equality and legal action may be taken. However, if you want to recruit people from minority groups, including women, you can take positive action to do this.

British Rail are aiming to recruit 5,000 women train drivers by 1999 to help replace 11,000 mostly male drivers who will retire by then. Part of their recruitment drive includes a package for improving recruitment and training practices and changing recruitment procedures and working hours, pay and conditions.

In 1992, up to thirty undergraduates from ethnic minority backgrounds were offered work placements with Midland Bank during the summer. Students on this scheme who were in their final year were guaranteed an initial interview for places on the bank's graduate training programme.

INVESTIGATE

- *Does your organization provide application forms for potential job-holders? If so, do the design of the form and the headings it uses come up to standard?*

Recruiting staff outside the UK

If you are recruiting staff abroad, there are a number of factors of which you need to be aware. These include:

- knowledge about local labour markets in the country in which you are recruiting;
- knowledge of local education systems and the status of educational qualifications;
- the need to consider language and cultural differences in an interview situation;
- avoiding the use of recruitment methods which are accepted in the UK but are counter to other cultures.

Once you have attracted the right candidates, you move into the next phase of recruitment, which is the selection of the right person for the job, covered in Chapter 3.

Legal and regulatory framework

There are certain actions which a potential employer may not take, governed by employment legislation. Further legislation is likely to be introduced by the European Commission. The summary below only concerns current UK-based law and is subject to change. If you are responsible for recruiting staff and for making decisions about any of the issues outlined in the summary, you should seek professional advice about current employment law.

The law concerning recruitment

Equal Pay Act 1970 (as amended); Equal Pay (Amendment) Regulations 1983

Women and men must receive equal pay for like work, work which is broadly similar, work rated as equal under a job evaluation scheme and work of equal value.

The Equal Pay Act 1970 was amended as a result of the Sex Discrimination Act of 1975 to provide for the inclusion of an equality clause in every woman's contract of employment. This equality clause is to make provision for modification of any term which, in a man's contract for the same work in the same company, is more favourable or beneficial except in cases such as compliance with laws regarding employment of a woman or where women are afforded special treatment concerning pregnancy or childbirth.

As with most legal requirements, this one is surrounded by exceptions, particularly the issue of 'material difference'. For example, a woman may be able to show that the work she does is broadly similar to that of a male colleague (or vice-versa) but the other person may still be eligible for higher pay if the jobs require specific qualifications and one person has higher qualifications than another.

Rehabilitation of Offenders Act 1974

Where a person who has been convicted of an offence and has served a sentence not exceeding thirty months in custody, has rehabilitated him or herself, he/she must be treated as if the offence had never been committed. This means that the candidate is not obliged to reveal any such sentence to a prospective employer. Certain categories of employee, including accountants, lawyers, teachers, those in the medical profession and those who work with persons under the age of 18 can be asked to disclose any previous offences.

Sex Discrimination Acts 1975 and 1986

Employers must not discriminate against women (or men) or married persons in the way in which they set about recruitment or make their selection arrangements and decisions.

Race Relations Act 1976

Employers must not discriminate against candidates on grounds of their race, colour, creed or ethnic origin unless they are following a policy of positive action.

Disabled Persons (Employment) Acts 1944 and 1958

Companies employing twenty or more staff are required to employ a quota of disabled people, currently 3 per cent of the total workforce. If the figure drops below this level, the employer must seek a permit from the Department of Employment to allow him/her to recruit further non-disabled staff.

Fair Employment (NI) Act 1989

Employers in Northern Ireland must not discriminate against candidates on religious grounds, most specifically because they are catholics or protestants.

Employment Act 1990

Employers must not discriminate against candidates on grounds of trade union membership or non-membership of a trade union.

Discrimination in recruitment advertising

Both the Equal Opportunities Commission and the Commission for Racial Equality publish codes of practice which include recommendations about advertising jobs. You should get current copies of these if you are involved in drawing up job advertisements. In summary, the Codes suggest that:

1 Employers should not confine advertisements unjustifiably to those areas or publications which would exclude or disproportionately reduce the numbers of applicants of a particular racial group.
2 Employers should avoid prescribing requirements such as length of residence or experience in the UK, and, where a particular qualification is required, it should be made clear that a fully comparable qualification obtained overseas is as acceptable as a UK qualification. Unless the sex or race of candidates is a GOQ for a particular job (see below), advertisements should make it clear that both men and women may apply.

General Occupational Qualifications (GOQs)

For some specific jobs, the sex or race of applicants has been agreed to be a GOQ and advertisements for these jobs are exempt from the Race Relations and Sex Discrimination Acts. These include some jobs which involve single-sex decency or privacy (e.g. toilet attendants), jobs in single-sex establishments (e.g. in single-sex hospitals), where there are legal restrictions on either men or women holding a job and for some jobs abroad; they also include jobs which involve participation in dramatic performance and some jobs in culture-specific restaurants. However, you should always check whether sex and/or race are, indeed, an accepted GOQ for the job in question.

Summary

The staff you recruit during the 1990s are likely to be with you into the twenty-first century. They are likely to have to cope with increasing change and flexibility in their jobs, to have to acquire new skills and take on different responsibilities. As a manager, you are going to have to plan for future staffing levels.

A good organizational strategy is one which links the recruitment of staff with their development and retention and which includes short- and long-term staffing requirements. In order to determine future staffing needs, you should consider auditing the current skills and knowledge of existing employees (Human Resource Auditing). This includes analysing existing jobs and determining future skill requirements.

Whether you are carrying out a Human Resource Audit or filling a job vacancy, you will need to draw up a job description which includes the title of the job, its main purpose and scope and the main tasks involved in its performance. From this you can prepare an employee specification which specifies the essential and desirable qualities required in the jobholder; these include the relevant skills, knowledge, experience and attitudes necessary to perform the job.

Recruitment of suitable candidates may take place internally or externally and can be undertaken in a number of ways. The commonest of these, particularly for external candidates, is by advertising. Any advertisement needs to be designed to attract the attention, interest and desire of potential applicants, and lead them to take action to apply. It also needs to give essential information about the job, act as a filter for unsuitable candidates and conform with the legislation governing unlawful discrimination. Finally, you need to decide on which form(s) of application you will use and prepare a comprehensive set of 'further particulars' for enquirers.

Activities

1

Job analysis Using two or more of the methods suggested in this chapter, choose the job of someone for whom you have responsibility and conduct a job analysis.

2

Job description Draw up a job description, based on the job analysis you have just conducted.

3

Employee specification From the job description, draw up an employee specification under the headings suggested in this chapter.

4

Recruitment advertising Design a recruitment advertisement from the job description and employee specification which will attract the right candidates.

5

Application forms Design an application form for the job in question which will provide you with the information you need to make a decision about whether or not to short-list individuals for the selection process.

References

Herriot, P. (1989) *Recruitment in the 90s*, Institute of Personnel Management, London

Pearson, R. (1991) *The Human Resource: Managing People and Work in the 1990s*, McGraw-Hill, Maidenhead

Schofield, P. (1992) Local government job ads: the good, the bad and the ugly. *Personnel Management*, April, pp. 41−4

Further reading

Herriot, P. (1989) *Recruitment in the 90s*, Institute of Personnel Management, London
Plumbley, P. (1985) *Recruitment and Selection*, Institute of Personnel Management, London

3 Selecting the right people

Introduction

As we said earlier, people are an expensive resource; it is worth taking time and effort to find the right person for the right job.

> The Director of Recruitment and Training with National Air Traffic Services has been quoted as saying, 'If the Civil Aviation Authority was able to improve its selection rate by just 1 per cent, it would save £250,000 annually.' (*Personnel Management*, August 1991, p. 9)

Selection can be defined as choosing the best person for the job from among candidates who come from within the organization or from outside. It involves setting up fair selection processes which, as far as possible, are designed to predict how an individual will behave at work and whether he or she can perform a specific range of tasks adequately. In this chapter, we look at the advantages and disadvantages of different methods of selection and give an overview of the selection process including:

- Short-listing candidates from application forms.
- Rejecting unsuccessful applicants.
- Interviewing candidates on a one-to-one basis and by a panel interview.
- Questioning techniques.
- Alternative methods of selection including, psychometric and psychological tests, the use of biodata and assessment centres.
- Legal and regulatory advice on non-discriminatory practice in selection.

Management in practice

Initial selection: drawing up a short-list

If you are faced with an enormous pile of applications, many of which seem to have come from candidates who do not have the essential qualities for the job, then your recruitment process has failed. Think how much that has cost you and other people in terms of your time; and how much more it is going to cost you in sorting through the applications, writing to unsuitable candidates and, perhaps, at the end of the day, having to start the whole process over again because you have failed to attract a suitable candidate. It is also bad practice because it has raised unrealistic expectations in the applicants that they might be suitable for the job you have advertised.

However, let us assume you followed the suggestions for good practice in Chapter 2 and that you have attracted a reasonable field of possible candidates. You now have to look at each application carefully and measure it against the 'essential' and 'desirable' qualities you identified in your employee specification.

Take the essential qualities first. Obviously, you should be interested in any candidates who fulfil all the essential requirements for the job, and less interested in those who only fulfil part of them. Selection also involves rejection. When it comes to rejecting applicants, it is both morally and practically right to let them know why they have been rejected. Look at the extracts from letters to unsuccessful applicants below and decide which you would rather receive if you were in their place.

'We were very interested in your application for the post of . . . in this organization, but are sorry to have to tell you that you have been unsuccessful in being short-listed.'

'Thank you for your application for the post of . . . but I am sorry that it has not been successful. There was a great deal of interest in this job and I am afraid we are not able to interview everyone.'

'Thank you for your application for the post of . . . As you know from the information we sent to you, we need someone who is a fluent German speaker since this particular job involves negotiating with managers in our branches in Bonn and Berlin, many of whom do not speak English. In your application, you state that you do not speak or read German and I am afraid that this is an essential part of the job.'

The blow — and any letter of rejection is a blow to the receiver's hopes and pride — is softened in the third example since there is a clear reason given why the person cannot fulfil the requirements of this particular job. It also demonstrates that your application form needs to pin-point the essential qualities of the job or you may be turning someone down on insufficient evidence. Since your recruitment procedure was designed to attract good applicants, you may be turning someone away who might have potential for another job in your organization. If you take time to write personal letters to unsuccessful candidates, both at this stage and after you have made a final decision between short-listed candidates, you will create goodwill in all applicants who will be encouraged to apply again in the future. Some organizations now insist on the completion of a form at this stage which gives individual reasons for not short-listing all applicants. If you do not give adequate reasons for not short-listing people for further selection, you run the risk of being accused − rightly or wrongly − of discrimination on grounds not related to the job in question.

Having rejected those applicants who do not fulfil your essential requirements, you may choose to offer the rest a chance of selection or, if the numbers are too great, continue to short-list on the basis of 'desirable' qualities. But this requires some kind of objective priority-setting: are any of these qualities more desirable than others? You may need to revise and prioritize your list of desirable qualities before making a final decision.

Once you have reduced your list of applicants to a manageable size, you may also want to call up references unless these were included with the application. If you have ever been asked to write a reference yourself, you will know how difficult it is, particularly for someone whose work is barely adequate or worse. If you fail to give a 'good' reference, that person will not get another job and you may be stuck with them. So treat references with caution; on a scale which measures the predictive validity of different selection methods, references rate just above astrology, graphology and chance.

The selection process

We mentioned this in Chapter 2. In order to let applicants know about the selection process, what form it will take and what will be required of them, you need to have designed this at the recruitment stage. What choices are open to you?

Obviously, the method or methods of selection you choose need to be able to predict future performance in the job as much as possible. But this is not always, or even generally, the reason why people choose one method over another. Other factors such as experience and cost-effectiveness also have an effect and, despite the evidence against them, interviews are still the most commonly used method.

INVESTIGATE

- *What selection methods are used in your organization?*

The interview

The selection interview has had a bad press; from 1920 onwards, psychologists and management researchers have demonstrated that interviews are both unreliable and invalid as predictors of future performance. They have proved that:

- Interviewers often make up their minds about a candidate within the first five minutes of the interview and − consciously or unconsciously − spend the rest of the interview trying to justify their judgement.
- Interviewers' judgements of candidates can be affected by their appearance, speech, gender and race either positively or negatively; people tend to favour others whom they perceive to be like themselves.
- Few interviewers have undertaken any training in interview skills.
- Research on memory shows that we remember information we hear at the beginning and end of an interview and, thus, tend to forget vital details and facts given in the middle.
- It is impossible for the human brain to concentrate at the same level over a prolonged period; thus if you are interviewing several candidates on the same day, they may not receive equal amounts of your attention.
- Finally, the British Psychological Society has found that even well-conducted interviews are only 25 per cent better than choosing someone by sticking a pin in a list of candidates!

Despite all the evidence against interviews, they remain the most widely used method of selection for two reasons: first, they are relatively inexpensive, and secondly, many people feel a strong need to meet and talk to someone before appointing them. So, if you decide that an interview is going to be part of your selection process, you will need to make it as reliable and valid a method as possible. There are four main factors which can affect the success or failure of a selection interview:

1 The amount of preparation before the interview.
2 The conduct and form of the interview.
3 The kinds of questions the interviewer asks.
4 The quality of the final decision-making process.

1 Preparation

A large part of the necessary preparation for the interview should already have been carried out by drawing up an employee specification and matching applications against this. However, it is unlikely that there is a perfect match against all the essential and desirable qualities in your employee specification and there is a need to identify individual candidates' strengths and weaknesses in the interview. There may also be information available on how candidates have performed in other selection methods, such as those outlined later in this chapter; information on their achievements in assessment centres for example, or results of psychometric testing. All relevant information on each candidate should be collected and analysed before interviews take place (Figure 3.1).

> A Health Authority were taken to court for not interviewing a well-qualified black nursing officer. They were unable to prove that the applicant did not fulfil the requirements of the post because they had not drawn up an employee specification.

You will need to identify which areas you need to question in detail from what you already know about the candidate's relevant skills, knowledge, experience and attitudes; and the important word there is 'relevant'. It is easy in the interview itself to be side-tracked into discussions of common interest or enthusiasm and to forget about more important issues.

Your objective at the interview is to obtain as much relevant and accurate information about the candidate as possible as objectively as possible and you also need to second-guess what kinds of questions candidates are likely to ask. These might include questions about salary scales, career progression, opportunities for staff training and development, holiday entitlement and so on. As the interviewer you will need to be prepared, as far as possible, to give the answers.

There are also some physical aspects of the interview which need to be considered, including:

- Where it will be held.
- Who will meet and look after the candidates.

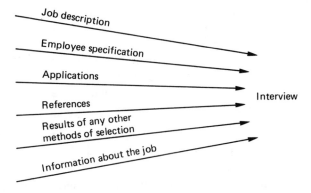

Figure 3.1 Information you need before the interview

- What refreshments may be needed for both candidates and interviewers.
- How the seating should be arranged to put candidates at their ease.
- How the candidates can claim travel expenses.

Unless you aim to put candidates at their ease, you will not get the best out of them. Some organizations hold what are called 'stress interviews', designed to put candidates under pressure in order that the interviewer can see how they react, but there are serious ethical considerations here.

Any interview should be arranged so that you and other interviewers are free from interruptions, telephone calls or 'urgent' messages; it is patently unfair on candidates if you or others are frequently switching attention away from the interview to deal with other matters and it gives a poor impression of your managerial competence. Remember that the candidate is likely to be feeling apprehensive about the interview and try to arrange the seating so that it is as informal as possible; avoid sitting behind a table or a desk since this immediately creates a barrier between you and the person being interviewed. Also, try not to sit with your back to a window as this creates a 'silhouette' effect which can be disturbing. When the candidate arrives or is shown in, start by trying to put him or her at ease; do not launch straight into the interview itself. Spend a few moments on general and 'safe' issues such as how the candidate got there or the weather.

> 'When I got to the place, I was shown into a room with several other people and asked to wait. It was really embarrassing. We all knew we'd come after the same job so we didn't look at each other – imagine six or seven people staring at spaces on the wall because they didn't want anyone to think they were looking at them. I had to wait for fifty minutes; they must have told everyone to come at the same time.
>
> 'When I went into the manager's office, he had this huge desk and I had to sit in front of it. It was like being back at school and I felt I'd done something wrong before I even started. He didn't smile at me, or even say "Good morning," just "Why do you want this job?" It was so unexpected, my mind just went blank. I didn't get the job but I wouldn't have wanted to work there anyway.'
> (job applicant)

2 Form and conduct of the interview

Your main decision in this area is about who should be involved in the actual interviews. Interviews may be conducted:

- on a one-to-one-basis;
- as a succession of one-to-one interviews;
- by an interview panel or board; or by
- a combination of the above.

INVESTIGATE

- *What kind, or kinds of selection interviewing does your organization practise?*

One-to-one interviews are less threatening to potential candidates than panel or board interviews but they have disadvantages in that each interviewer has no opportunity to listen to candidates' answers to the other people involved. Large panels (of more than four or five) allow less time for individual questioning and demand more time when it comes to making selection decisions; they are also very threatening to candidates. However, recent research on the interview as a method of selection indicates that panel interviews are the best approach in terms of the validity of decisions made but least popular with candidates. Whatever form of interview you decide to use, if it involves other people they will need to have all the essential information about the candidate beforehand and they should meet to discuss how they will handle the main areas of questioning. They should also agree on the conduct of the interview.

If there is to be a panel or board, it will need a Chair who will be responsible for welcoming and introducing each candidate and for ensuring that all the major points have been covered by the other members of the panel. The Chair will also be responsible for ensuring that the final decision is made and communicated to the successful and unsuccessful candidates.

In some organizations, candidates are interviewed by more than one panel, in which case, each panel needs to be chaired.

Some selection specialists advocate complex scoring systems based on point systems like those devised by Rodger (1952) (Seven Point Plan) or Fraser (1978) (Five-fold Grading System), but any scoring system needs to relate closely to those qualities you identified in the employee specification. In many people's opinion, both Rodger's and Fraser's systems have serious defects and are open to discriminatory practices. You might like to devise a scoring system based on the specification but you should consult with, and agree the ratings with, other interviewers beforehand. It can be an aid to objectivity if properly designed, agreed and adhered to; too often, individual preferences and bias overtake objective ratings.

3 Questioning

Your preparation and discussion with other people involved in the interview process should have identified the areas you need to question for each candidate. There are ways of asking questions that will elicit the answers you require and there are also questions you should not ask.

Not unnaturally, many candidates are nervous when they come for an interview and have some difficulty in putting themselves across. You can help them in the way you phrase your questions. You can make a choice, depending on what kind of answer you are looking for, between any of the following:

- **Open questions** – which are designed to draw the candidate out such as, 'Will you tell me about how you set up a networking system in your last job?' or 'Can you tell me more about this training course you went on last year?' or 'What appeals to you about this job?'
- **Closed questions** – used to clarify a point of fact and which often only require a short or single word answer. For example, 'Did you head up the team?' or 'Was that your own idea?' or 'Did you or your employer decide to do that?'
- **Hypothetical questions** – which can be used to find out how a candidate might respond in certain situations such as 'If we offered you this job, how would you go about improving communications between departments?' or 'If you had a budget of £100,000 for promoting a new product, how would you spend it?'
- **Probing questions** – which are necessary if you feel a candidate has not given you a full answer and you want to find out more. They can be used immediately after a candidate has referred to something you would like to know more about by saying 'Exactly what happened next ...?' or you can return to an earlier point by saying, for example, 'I'd like to go back to something you said earlier about not enjoying your work on the project team. Could you tell me why you didn't enjoy it?'

Questions you should not ask include those of a personal nature which are not relevant to the job and/or could be described as discriminatory. For example:

- 'How old are you?'
- 'Are you married? What does your partner do?'
- 'What religious holidays do you observe?'

- 'What arrangements do you have for child care?'

The Commission for Racial Equality and the Equal Opportunities Commission both have information about basic principles of non-discriminatory questioning in selection interviews and some of these are outlined later in the section on legal and regulatory frameworks.

Do not ask questions which are likely to take the candidate a long time to answer such as 'Tell me about your previous jobs ...'. Try to avoid asking multiple questions such as 'I'd like you to tell me about your work with the Research and Development Group. Was it interesting, what did you find most satisfying about it and what did you like least?' The candidate will be confused and will probably only answer part of the question. Avoid questions, too, which are designed to give you the answer you want rather than the real answer, such as 'Wouldn't it have been more efficient if you had brought in a specialist to deal with that part of the job?' or 'You don't like working on your own, do you?'

Ideally, the candidate should do most of the talking so avoid getting into interesting discussions of your pet subject or reminiscences of your own experiences. Do not probe on sensitive or emotional issues unless these are truly relevant to the job.

An interviewing technique which uses examples from the candidate's own past experience to focus on the skills needed for another job is called **behavioural interviewing**. For example, if you had analysed a job which you felt required quick decision-making, the ability to work under pressure and the need for diplomatic handling of problems you might ask questions like the following:

- 'Give me an example of a time when you had to make a decision quickly.'
- 'Can you describe any job you have held where you were faced with problems and pressures which tested your ability to cope?'
- 'Can you give me an example of a time when you had to conform to a policy with which you did not agree?'

Some candidates, often through nervousness, will talk endlessly and pointlessly if given the chance. You will need to bring them back to the point courteously, perhaps rephrase the question or move on to another area. It is perfectly acceptable for you and other interviewers to take notes during the interview; in fact it is preferable if you are interviewing more than one person on the same day. It is a good idea to explain to the candidates that you intend to do this as an aid to decision-making, but try not to make your note-taking obvious, particularly when probing sensitive areas.

When you have asked all the questions you feel are necessary, you should give each candidate an opportunity to ask questions of you and other interviewers. Do not be surprised if they cannot think of any; again, nervousness and the effort of concentrating on your questions may have caused them to forget what they wanted to ask. You might even make some suggestions such as 'Is there anything you would like to ask us about the job itself, or the organization? Anything about wages or holidays or shift hours or . . .?' Of course, most of this information should have been covered in your Information Pack but candidates may have concerns which they need to raise at this point.

You should be careful not to make promises to candidates which cannot be fulfilled, such as assurances about training and promotion if they take the job. Apart from being morally wrong to promise something which, later, cannot be provided, employees will be resentful if they feel they took the job under false pretences. Sometimes, interviewers are so keen to appoint a particularly outstanding candidate that they make offers, often in good faith, to encourage the person to join the organization; later, when the offers do not materialize, the dissatisfied employee may feel bitter enough to make a formal complaint.

Finally, when closing the interview, thank the candidates for coming and let them know when and how they can expect to learn the outcome.

4 Making a decision

Despite all your efforts at obtaining the best range of candidates, briefing other interviewers and controlling the interview itself, it is likely that when it comes to making a choice out of say, six candidates, that different interviewers will have made different choices. If your recruitment and short-listing processes have been effective, this is inevitable since the choice will have been narrowed down to a few very good candidates. The decision-making process needs to be managed in the same way as the other elements of recruitment and selection since the eventual judgement is the culmination of all that has gone before. It has to be rational, explicable and unbiased and based as far as possible on objective criteria.

One way of looking at this process is by analysing why you would NOT appoint certain candidates – this is useful since you should explain to unsuccessful candidates the reasons why they were not selected and, again, your organization may require these reasons to be given in writing for their own records. Here, your employee specification and analysis of essential and desirable qualities for performance of the job should be used as your benchmarks.

Once a decision has been reached, the successful candidate should be offered the job and those who were unsuccessful need to be told. Again, bear in mind that these unsuccessful candidates might be successful in future and give as much feedback as possible as to why each failed to get the job. Remember, too, that a verbal acceptance of a job is not legally binding and, until the candidate has formally accepted a job offer in writing, he or she might change their mind.

INVESTIGATE

- *Think back to a selection interview in which you were involved. How far did it reflect the 'good practice' suggested here?*

Other selection methods

Alternative or complementary methods of selection include a range of psychometric tests, the use of biodata and the use of assessment centres. In addition, there are a number of less well known and less reliable methods involving the analysis of handwriting, astrology and honesty testing (or lie detecting). Self-assessment and peer assessment have also been used but are also considered to be unreliable.

Research has shown that psychometric tests, which include work sampling, tests of ability and personality tests, can be more reliable than interviewing providing the test is relevant to the job which has to be performed and that the tester has been trained in its use. Biodata, which is short for 'biographical data' is a relatively recent selection technique which appears to have high predictive validity and can be cost-effective; however, it is more suitable for organizations who have a large number of vacancies for the same type of job and it does require specialist training in its administration. Assessment centres are not places but processes, involving candidates being assessed on various job-related tests by a range of assessors. They are considered to be valid, reliable and fair as a means of selecting people and, again, require trained assessors.

Psychometric testing

There is a vast range of tests available on the open market and one must be cautious in assessing their predictive value. Some large organizations who rely heavily on testing in their selection and promotion procedures are finding that different departments are using different tests and that decisions are being made independently of any corporate strategy. Similarly, only chartered occupational psychologists are qualified to train people in applying and analysing most worthwhile tests and there is a growth in amateur consultancy and 'easy to use, no training required' short personality tests in this area; these are usually unreliable.

> Undergraduates and others who are attending a number of job selections which involve aptitude and personality tests, have often carried out the same test several times before. Experience shows that individuals' performance on aptitude tests improves significantly when they undergo the same, or similar, tests more than once.

However, testing is still relatively rare. In looking at recent advances in psychometric testing, Smith et al (1989) suggest that about 5 per cent of job applicants are given some kind of test, although the percentage is likely to be higher in the case of management jobs and is also higher in sales jobs and in the transport industry.

Psychological tests

These include ability tests, covering both physical and mental ability, personality tests and tests of motivation. In some cases, they may also include tests of a medical or fitness nature.

> After the Canon Street rail crash, in which the driver of the train was proved to have taken cannabis, British Rail negotiated with the transport union RMT to introduce pre-employment drug tests for safety-related jobs.

Ability tests usually focus on mental abilities such as verbal, numerical and spatial abilities and specific tests have been developed for computer programmers, systems analysts, people working on word processors and those who work in automated offices.

> The Civil Aviation Authority, which recruits over 200 people a year as air traffic controllers, uses computer-based simulation as part of their recruitment and selection process.

Recent developments in ability testing have increased their sensitivity to individual levels of ability and the more sophisticated ones can be used to differentiate between adequate and higher-level candidates.

Personality tests relate to, for example, the degree to which a person can be categorized as extrovert or introvert, as stable or neurotic, as dependent or independent. It is the author's opinion that there needs to be a clear rationale for asking candidates to undertake a personality test as part of the selection process unless (a) the outcome of the test(s) is essential to predicting adequate performance in the job, (b) the test is proved to be non-discriminatory in terms of gender, race, creed or disability and (c) the person who is administering and analysing the results has been professionally trained.

Work sampling is a test which attempts to replicate some of the key elements of a job. Such tests are expensive to design unless they are going to be widely used since each work-sample has to be related to a specific job. Examples of work-sample tests for managers include:

- in-tray prioritizing exercises;
- group problem-solving exercises;
- consensus decision-making;
- role play simulations.

Assessment centres, which are discussed below, use very similar tests.

Biodata

Biodata methods of selection are relatively new and are based on the assumption that details of people's lives and experiences will reveal their personality and aptitudes. Candidates have to answer a very detailed questionnaire which is then scored and selection decisions are based on the scoring. They are used effectively for filtering very large numbers of applicants applying for a single job or for entry-level jobs such as management trainees. In the case of small numbers of applicants or a wide range of jobs, however, biodata can be an extremely expensive exercise.

Assessment centres

Assessment centres are considered to be valid, reliable and fair and a survey conducted in the mid-1980s found that 21 per cent of companies used assessment centres or assessment centre exercises to select staff at managerial level. Assessment centre exercises are derived from detailed job analysis and may include:

- group role play in which each candidate plays an assigned role, such as production manager, sales manager, finance director;

- in-tray prioritizing exercises;
- problem-solving and presentations;
- analytical and reporting exercises.

Candidates are evaluated by a number of assessors on their perform-ance in these exercises. The resulting data are then evaluated and scores are derived for each candidate. These methods are now being widely used for appraisal and promotion within organizations as well as for selection purposes, which increases their cost-effectiveness to the organization.

These alternative methods of selection are useful in initially screen-ing large numbers of candidates prior to a second stage, which may include interviews. They can provide additional information about candidates prior to final selection but, with the exception of assess-ment centres, they are rarely predictive enough in themselves. They should never be used unless they relate directly to the job role concerned and, in most cases, they require a trained professional to analyse the results.

INVESTIGATE

- *Does your organization use any of these alternative methods of selection? Are they administered by trained staff?*

Legal and regulatory framework

It is against the law to discriminate in the way in which candidates are assessed for selection. Discrimination may be either direct or indirect.

Direct discrimination includes:

- Specifying different assessment criteria for men and women which are not justified.
- Deliberately setting out to exclude people of either sex or from ethnic minority groups.

Indirect discrimination includes:

- Setting criteria for selection which disadvantage women and people from ethnic minority groups.
- Using tests which cannot be directly linked to performance of the particular job.

- Requiring women to undertake tests of physical strength which men are not asked to undertake.
- Asking questions of women which are not asked of all candidates.
- Rejecting a female candidate on the grounds of her pregnancy.

Good practice in interviewing

The Equal Opportunities Commission and the Commission for Racial Equality have set out some basic principles for selection interviewing, summarized below:

- The same kinds of questions should be asked across all racial groups and to both men and women.
- Questions should all be relevant to the job description and employee specification.
- Interviewers should avoid questions related to their perceptions of different cultures, although they need to be aware of religious and cultural differences in candidates.
- Questions should not be based on assumptions about traditional women's roles in the home and family.

The Employers' Forum on Disability have also produced guidance on disability etiquette in interviewing. This includes:

- Conducting interviews with disabled people as you would with anyone else.
- Emphasizing abilities, achievements and individual qualities but avoiding putting people with disabilities on a pedestal.
- Remembering that questions concerning a candidate's disability should be restricted to those relevant to the job.
- Not making assumptions about a candidate's ability to perform certain tasks.
- Not relying on intermediaries for information or opinions about a disabled candidate's capacity to perform the job; using your own judgement from discussion with the candidate.
- Not requiring application forms, letters etc. to be handwritten unless this is essential to performance of the job.

In proving discrimination in selection methods, the onus is on the applicant to make a case. The following example, which came to the Court of Appeal in 1991, illustrates this.

Ms King, an ethnic Chinese, applied for a job with the Great Britain–China Centre. Despite meeting all the selection criteria in the advertisement, she was not invited for interview. When challenged, the Centre said that she had failed to meet other criteria which had been established after all the responses were received. In coming to its conclusion that Ms King had been discriminated against on grounds of race, the industrial tribunal used the facts that although one-sixth of the applicants were ethnic Chinese, none of them had been called for interview and the Centre in fact employed no Chinese person. The tribunal further felt that the additional criteria which Ms King failed to meet had been established and used to justify unlawful discrimination rather than being genuine requirements for the job. (*The Personnel Manager's Factbook*, 1992)

Summary

If you followed the advice in Chapter 2, your carefully worded advertisement and comprehensive information pack for candidates should have produced a degree of self-selection before you receive genuine applications for the job you have to fill. This was the intention. However, it is highly probable that you have too many applicants for the job and that you are going to have to decide upon appropriate ways for selecting the right person. You are probably going to have to make an initial selection on the basis of the written applications you have received, matched with the employee specification. Thereafter, there are a range of selection techniques from which you can choose for carrying out the next stage. Finally, you have to make a decision on the basis of whichever selection technique(s) you have used.

This process will help you to assess and select candidates against team and organizational requirements. The first stage will be concerned with evaluating all the information available to you prior to selection, including the job description and employee specification, application forms, CVs, references and, where available, results of any tests which candidates may have undergone in the selection process. You will have to determine the cost-effectiveness and suitability of applying particular selection methods in choosing the right person for the job and agree the selection criteria. You will also have to agree who will be involved in any interviews you plan to hold and make arrangements for briefing and discussing the process with other interviewers. During the process, there will be a certain amount of record-keeping, including communication to successful and unsuccessful candidates, and you will need to be familiar with current legislation concerning selection, salary levels within the labour market, commencement dates and other financial details related to the job vacancy.

The amount of care and effort you have put into all the stages of the recruitment and selection process should be reflected in the quality of the person you finally select.

Activities

1 Imagine that you have been asked to take part in or lead a selection interview for a post in your area of responsibility. Choose a particular post and note down the essential questions you would ask candidates.

---

2 Write a short letter to an unsuccessful candidate who was short-listed for a post but failed to be appointed. How would you word such a letter so that the candidate felt that he or she had been given a fair assessment?

References

Fraser, M. (1978) *Employment Interviewing*, MacDonald and Evans, London
The Personnel Manager's Factbook (1992) Gee
Rodger, A. (1952) *The Seven Point Plan*, National Institute of Industrial Psychology, Paper No. 1
Smith, M., Gregg, M. and Andrews, D. (1989) *Selection and Assessment: A New Appraisal*, Pitman, London

Further reading

Anstey, E. (1977) *An Introduction to Selection Interviewing*, HMSO, London
Bray, T. (1992) *The Selection Maze*, Mercury
Breakwell, G. M. (1990) *Interviewing*, British Psychological Society/Routledge, London
Smith, M., Gregg, M. and Andrews, D. (1989) *Selection and Assessment: A New Appraisal*, Pitman, London
Toplis, J., Dalewicz, V. and Fletcher, C. (1987) *Psychological Testing: A Practical Guide*, Institute of Personnel Management, London

4 Managing people as individuals

Introduction

On any day as a manager, you are likely to have to 'manage' other people on a one-to-one basis. This involves understanding people as individuals and recognizing their differences as well as drawing up some general principles for managing them.

As managers, we need to understand why people choose to perform satisfactorily or unsatisfactorily; why some people appear to be committed to their jobs and others are often absent or unwell. We need to find out what rewards and incentives individuals value so that, where possible, we can provide these. In short, we need to provide motivation for the people for whom we are responsible.

In this chapter, we will be looking at some of the ways in which that motivation can be provided and how you, as a manager, can get the best out of your staff. This will include:

- Explanations of why people behave as they do.
- Motivation and reward systems at work.
- Delegation.
- Listening to people.
- Counselling people at work.
- Equal opportunities.
- Managing interpersonal conflict.
- Health and safety in the workplace.
- The legal and regulatory framework.

Management in practice

Individuals at work

What do you think about the other people you work with – your boss, your subordinates and your colleagues? How do you know that the way you think about other people is shared by them? And what is their opinion about you? To manage people effectively, you need to clear your mind of your own beliefs, opinions and assumptions since they are highly personal to you. You and your boss may have quite different ideas about how A performs his or her job or how reliable B is, and these may be different again from the ideas of some of your colleagues. Nobody is necessarily 'right' or 'wrong' in their opinions, providing these are based on facts rather than on personal beliefs. Think of some of the idiosyncratic ways people think about others.

'I never trust anyone who wears brightly coloured ties.'

'She's got two young children so she'll always be asking for time off.'

'He's joined the same golf club as Simon − must be looking for promotion.'

'You should see her desk − it's a tip. I'd never ask her to take on organizing anything serious.'

You could say some of these statements were based on 'facts', but they are hardly objective, nor do the opinions stated necessarily follow from the observations.

INVESTIGATE

• *Think back to any recent discussions you have had with other people at work. Did any of them make statements like those above? Did you?*

Wrightsman, in his book *Assumptions about Human Nature* (1974), identified six categories of belief on which people based their assumptions about others. These are given below and you might like to try to place your own beliefs about other people in relation to each category.

Wrightsman stated that everyone had certain general beliefs about other people and the degree to which they were trustworthy, unselfish, nonconformist (or independent) and rational. They also believed other people shared their values (or not) and that, in general, others were fairly simple, or fairly complex, human beings (Figure 4.1).

	1	2	3	4	5	
Trustworthy						Untrustworthy
Unselfish						Selfish
Nonconformist						Conformist
Rational						Irrational
Same values						Different values
Simple						Complex

Figure 4.1 Wrightsman's five-point scale of beliefs

INVESTIGATE

- *If you identified your own set of beliefs using Wrightsman's categories, you might like to try them out on someone else and see how closely you match each other's ways of thinking about other people.*

Another reason why people behave differently in a work situation is, quite simply, because they have different abilities and experience. In the previous chapter, you considered assessment centres as a form of selection; assessment centres and other tests measure ability which differentiates one individual from another. Some people will always rate 'better' than others in terms of mental or physical ability. They may not choose to use that ability at work, perhaps because they find the job unsatisfying, boring or beneath their ability, or because it does not allow them to use a particular area of ability. My son once scored extremely highly on a test of spatial ability, yet has never had a job in which he could use this particular talent.

However, the identification of a particular level of ability does not mean that you can predict how that person will behave at work although it has been proved that most top managers are of above average intelligence – but not in the genius class (Hunt, 1979). It is just another piece of the jigsaw that makes up an individual. Another, more complex piece, is the kind of experience the individual has had. If you think about it, we have all had individual experiences of life before and outside work. Some of these may appear to be similar, such as the type of school attended, or the kind of houses people live in, but most of each individual's experience will be specific to that person. Everyone brings with them a whole clutch of different experiences which affect how they behave and perform at work.

Experience at work also affects how people behave. Take the example of a meeting between, say, the production manager, the sales manager and the company accountant. A discussion might go as follows:

Sales manager: I'm getting a lot of complaints from customers about our long delivery times – we're going to lose out to the competition. Mitchells can guarantee delivery in 10 days; we're lucky if the customer gets stuff from us under three weeks. You've got to increase production or we'll all be looking for new jobs.

Production manager: That's all very well. I can't increase production until we get two new machines and the people to operate them – it's as simple as that. Give me the machines and the staff – you'll get your shorter delivery.

Accountant: 'We can't afford new machines at the moment — you know that. Not until sales pick up, and the current figures aren't promising. You'll need to get your sales staff working harder . . .'

Deadlock. Each person has a perfectly valid argument, yet they are each approaching the problem from the different viewpoints of their work experience. People can also find difficulty when they change from one organization to another where the 'cultures' of those organizations are different. Someone who has worked, for example, in the Civil Service, which is highly structured and where there are rules and procedures to be followed for nearly every activity, would find it difficult to adjust to working in a voluntary organization where there is great stress on consultation and participation, even if the requirements of the job were broadly similar; their work experience would be quite different.

We all make assumptions about other people based on our own experience — it is a way of making sense of relating to others. We each set ourselves certain standards and expect other people to adhere to them, even though they may not share our views and have different standards for themselves.

Motivation

Motivation has become one of the buzz-words of modern management. 'He lacks motivation', 'Jo really motivates her team — they'll do anything for her', 'We need to motivate the workforce . . .'. Yet, like all human states, motivation is both highly individual and complex and there is a difference between what motivates people to perform above average and what leads to below-average performance.

Assumptions about the way people behave at work

Based on his observations of management during his years as a senior administrator in an American college, Professor Douglas McGregor suggested that managers make either Theory X or Theory Y assumptions about the way others behave. (The terms Theory X or Y are merely names McGregor (1960) used to describe the kinds of assumptions.) Theory X assumptions include the following:

- that the average human being inherently dislikes work and will avoid it if possible;
- that, because of this, subordinates must be coerced, controlled, directed or threatened with punishment to get them to put in adequate effort at work;
- that the average person prefers to be directed, wishes to avoid responsibility, has relatively little ambition and wants security above all else.

Perhaps you know of managers who have all or some of these assumptions about the people who work for them; perhaps you yourself think about some other people in this way. Theory X has had its followers for a long time and can certainly be used for explaining some kinds of behaviour in organizations. More recent research on people at work, however, supports McGregor's set of Theory Y assumptions which include the following:

* that most people do not inherently dislike work and that, according to the conditions, it may be either a source of satisfaction or punishment;
* that people will generally exercise self-direction and self-control in pursuit of objectives to which they are committed;
* that most people learn, under proper conditions, not only to accept but to seek responsibility;
* that most people are not being used by organizations to their full potential;
* that, in order to obtain commitment from employees, rewards should fulfil an individual's self-actualization needs (we will be looking at self-actualization later in this chapter).

If managers choose either the set of assumptions associated with Theory X or with Theory Y, there will be a tendency throughout the organization for people to respond to the way they are managed. Therefore, if employees feel that they are not being trusted, they may behave in a less trustworthy way.

INVESTIGATE

* *Can you think of any examples of employees behaving in Theory X or Theory Y ways and relate this behaviour to their manager's or supervisor's assumptions about them?*

The Theory Y explanation of the way we may think about other people at work included a belief about the kinds of rewards which people value. Frederick Taylor, an engineer and the exponent of the idea of 'scientific management', stated 'What the workforce want from their employers beyond anything else is high wages and what employers want from their workforce most of all is low labour costs of manufacture ... the existence or absence of these two elements forms the best index to either good or bad management' (Taylor, 1947). We all know that this assumption is outdated; although wages and the level of pay for the job are an important factor in reward systems, we can all think of people who are underpaid and yet enjoy their work and perform it effectively.

Not everyone works harder in the hope of a pay rise or a bonus. Companies like British Nuclear Fuels have bowed to pressure to reduce the working week for manual workers from 39 hours to 35. Other organizations, particularly those in the food, drink and tobacco industries, now find it necessary to offer other benefits such as increased holiday entitlement which are not directly financial.

Motivation based on satisfying individual needs

An alternative explanation of human behaviour is put forward by the psychologist Maslow, who believed there were five levels of need which the individual sought to satisfy. The lowest of these included the basic physiological needs for food, drink and shelter; once these were satisfied, individuals needed to protect themselves against danger, threat and deprivation – safety needs. Thereafter, the levels of need rose through social needs, the need for self-esteem and status (ego needs) to the need for self-actualization (Figure 4.2). Maslow explained self-actualization as follows:

A musician must make music, an artist must paint, a poet must write, if he is to be ultimately happy. What a man can be, he must be. This need we may call self-actualization ... It refers to the desire for self-fulfilment, namely the tendency for him to become actualized in what he is potentially ... the desire to become more and more what one is, to become everything that one is capable of becoming. (Maslow, 1943)

Later researchers have questioned the hierarchical nature of Maslow's explanation but share in his belief that people work for

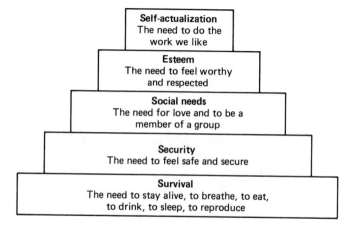

Figure 4.2 Maslow's hierarchy of needs

different reasons and that these reasons may include financial rewards but only as part of an overall reward system.

British Telecom offers its 6,000 managers a company-paid medical insurance scheme as part of their contract. Other employees can also participate in this scheme on a voluntary basis. The company also offers a selection of luxury items, including a personal organizer in a simulated bison-leather case, as part of its scheme for rewarding above-average performance.

Rank Xerox offers all its employees and their families company-paid medical insurance.

In America, corporate fitness schemes are having a dual effect on performance. Employees value participation in such schemes and, according to companies as diverse as Johnson and Johnson, NASA and the Dallas Police Department, both absenteeism rates and productivity have improved. Employees of Johnson and Johnson value the fitness programme for its opportunity to make social contact between employees at different levels in the organization.

Motivation and job satisfaction

Frederick Herzberg's research into the motivation of accountants and engineers revealed a number of factors which affected the way in which people felt about their work (Herzberg et al, 1959). These included:

- achievement
- recognition from others
- the work itself
- responsibility
- opportunities for advancement
- company policy and administration
- supervision
- salary
- inter-personal relations
- working conditions

Those factors which made people feel satisfied with their job and motivated them to work included high levels of achievement, recognition, opportunities for advancement and responsibility. The content of the work itself was also very important. Factors which affected employees adversely and which led them to feel dissatisfied with the work they were doing, included company policy and administration, supervision, salary, interpersonal relations and working conditions; if all or any of these were considered by individuals to be of a low standard, employees felt dissatisfied with what they were doing. Common symptoms of dissatisfaction at work include persistent lateness or absenteeism, below-average performance and real or imagined illness.

> In 1991, absenteeism in the UK was running at 370 million certified working days lost annually, estimated at costing British employers £6 billion.

The important lesson here is that if the factors classified by Herzberg as 'dissatisfiers' can be improved and the level of the 'satisfying' or motivating factors increased, performance should improve; merely improving the 'dissatisfiers' will not result in any long-term increase in an individual's motivation to work although it may produce short-term results and will increase job satisfaction.

Later researchers, such as Rosabeth Moss Kanter (1977), have examined the effect of job mobility and opportunity as motivators. For example, jobs that offer a clear career path, with opportunities for advancement and the acquisition of new skills and rewards, are likely to be more motivating than jobs in which the individual feels 'stuck' with no prospects of moving on.

There is considerable evidence to suggest that increasing employee involvement results in increasing the motivation to work in a particular organization. For example, the concept of Quality Circles was originally developed in Japan as a way of improving product quality. There, employee suggestion programmes are common and people are trained to analyze problems related to the quality of the product. Quality Circles are voluntary, regular meetings of about six to ten employees, all of whom share responsibility for a particular area of work, a particular work process, product or part of a product, or service. They are given time to discuss and solve quality problems with the aim of suggesting and implementing improvements. Not only do quality and productivity improve as a result, but those involved in Quality Circles become more highly motivated and have a greater awareness of work problems.

> In 1988, the *Guardian* newspaper asked its readers to participate in a survey entitled, 'Why Work?' and asked which factors were important in providing job satisfaction. Amongst those considered most important were:
>   personal freedom;
>   increased responsibility;
>   praise from superiors;
>   respect from others at work.
> 'Making money' appeared as twenty-eighth in order of importance.

INVESTIGATE

- *Why do you choose to work in your present job? List your reasons in order of importance. Then ask some of your colleagues and subordinates what their reasons are − they may well be different from yours.*

> Successful organizations such as Marks and Spencer and the John Lewis Partnership have long recognized that the job satisfaction of their employees is essential to their competitive advantage. Other organizations have also discovered this. For example, in a survey carried out by the contract caterer Compass in 1991, staff restaurants were found to be more highly valued than company cars as job benefits.

Having identified some general factors which can increase or decrease job satisfaction, it has to be recognized that each individual is likely to value these factors according to their own needs. For example, people with young children are likely to value the provision of childcare at work and flexible working hours more highly than people who do not have these responsibilities.

> When employees of Avon Cosmetics have been with the company for two years, they are eligible for vouchers towards the cost of childcare. These vouchers are given to staff with children under school age for the whole year, while those whose children are at school receive them for the school holiday periods.

> To help their employees with pre-school age children, Guys Hospital opened a new children's day nursery in 1992 with 40 places available for children of employees of Guys and Lewisham Trust, supported by contributions from the fast-food chain McDonalds.

These companies have concentrated on improving job satisfaction for employees with young children. But there are others whose dependants may be elderly or infirm, people whose partners may be ill, unemployed or in prison. There is a significant minority of people with no partners and who may or may not have dependants – all of these are unlikely to benefit from the very laudable childcare schemes offered by Avon, Guys and many other employers, yet they, too, have the right to increased job satisfaction. To a person who has a strong need for status, for example, an expensive company car is likely to bring satisfaction while another might value more free time to spend in leisure pursuits. In some cases, training incentives or a flexible retirement decade will increase job satisfaction and commitment to the organization.

> As incentives to its sales staff, Prudential Assurance offer all-expenses paid travel breaks and an annual dinner for its most successful salespeople.

It is essential that the 'reward' fulfils the individual's needs if motivation to work is to be maintained or increased. It is also necessary that the individual is convinced that, by putting in extra effort at work, his or her performance will be improved and that the reward he or she values will be forthcoming. Depending on your position as a manager and on the policies of the organization in which you work, it may be more or less difficult for you to ensure that an individual's needs can be fulfilled.

INVESTIGATE

● *What kinds of motivational rewards does your organization offer and how much influence can you have on providing appropriate rewards for above-average performance?*

Pay as a motivator

Herzberg identified the level of pay as one of the factors which could lead to dissatisfaction at work rather than one which contributed in any major way to job satisfaction and motivation. Yet, financial incentives are often the only reward organizations and their managers provide to induce increased performance. Performance-related pay systems can range from simple bonuses or salary/wage increases to more sophisticated pay systems such as time rates, payment by results (PBR), measured day work or profit sharing. Whatever the system, it is vital that it suits the circumstances of the organization and its ability to operate it successfully, and that it is participated in willingly by employees and their trade unions. It needs continual monitoring and evaluation to ensure it is fulfilling its purpose.

Woolwich Property Services were faced with the need to restructure their levels of pay, bonus policies and benefits with the slump in the property market in the early 1990s. This involved rationalizing the existing system of different basic salary levels and benefits whereby some staff would suffer pay cuts and others might lose or gain benefits such as a company car or car phone. The company produced a video and a booklet to explain the new system to all employees and each member of staff received an individual letter about changes to his or her salary and benefits. All levels of staff were fully briefed about the new system and, as far as management are aware, employees perceived it as fair even when they, personally, suffered reductions.

Profit-related pay schemes, whereby pay increases and bonuses are linked to organizational profits, have been slow to take off in the UK: in 1991, only 1,277 were in operation, covering 350,000 employees. However, the introduction of performance-related pay (PRP) in the 1980s has been more successful with almost 50 per cent of private-sector organizations operating PRP schemes for all non-manual staff in the early 1990s.

To be successful, performance-related pay schemes need to be based on performance management which links objectives, behaviours, competences and skills to organizational requirements. It needs to be fully understood by all employees who are affected by the scheme and, if possible, introduced with their agreement. On its own, a performance-related pay scheme can be unsuccessful; it should form part of an overall reward philosophy which meets individual and organizational needs.

The Archdiocese of Liverpool is considering the introduction of performance-related pay for some of its chaplains. Archbishop David Shepherd feels that there needs to be recognition of good performance in the service of the Church as there is in industry.

Lloyds Bank announced that, from April 1992, annual pay would be based on individual performance and that poor performers would not receive an increase.

Maslow, Herzberg and Moss Kanter all demonstrate that there is a wide range of factors which affect how people behave at work. Not all people will share beliefs in what is important to each of them as an individual, part of your task as a manager is to identify which factors affect which people and in what ways. We shall be continuing this theme in Chapter 9 on job design, an area where you can make practical changes to people's work in order to increase the motivating aspects of the job.

Delegating

The kinds of things that motivate people to work, as you have just seen, include having responsibility for the work they do. The particular job may hold certain responsibilities, but additional responsibility can be given by you, as the manager, through delegation. Not only can this free up your time for more important tasks, it can increase an individual's job satisfaction. But reluctant or poor delegation can be worse than no delegation at all.

Sandra knew she was taking on too much and was managing her time badly. Her manager had told her she must delegate more. 'Give young Lee a chance,' he said, 'he's a bright lad and could take on far more than he's doing at the moment. Why not ask him to take over organizing the roadshows this autumn?'

Sandra found the annual roadshows a chore because they involved so much time visiting venues, booking speakers and accommodation and checking out equipment. It seemed like a good idea and Lee was delighted to take them on. Sandra was still worried that he was not up to the job and that, if anything went wrong with the roadshows, she would be held responsible. She checked up on him continually, even telephoning the venues to make sure bookings had been made and insisting on seeing the letters he wrote to speakers. Eventually, there was a show-down

> when Lee discovered she had changed a booking he had made and upset all the arrangements for that particular roadshow as a result. He refused to work on the project any longer and Sandra had to take over herself, just as she was starting the annual appraisal system . . .

If you are going to delegate, do it properly. Choose someone whom you feel has the knowledge and ability to carry out the job. Brief them thoroughly and let them know just how much freedom and support they will have. You may feel you have to check up occasionally, but this should be done in a formal and agreed way, not behind the other person's back. Be prepared to relax your control as you gain confidence in the other person's performance. And remember to give them feedback on how they are doing.

Checklist for delegating

- What part(s) of my job can I delegate?
- What kinds of knowledge and ability are needed to carry out the delegated task(s)? Will any training be needed and is it available?
- Who could take on the job?
- What does that individual need to know about carrying out the job?
- How much personal support should I offer?
- What kind of formal reporting system should we set up to check on progress and how often should this be?
- What arrangements need to be made to give constructive feedback on the individual's performance?

If you keep the above questions in mind, the situation should not get out of hand to such an extent that you have to step in and do most of the work all over again yourself. If things do go wrong, you need to analyse the cause; perhaps the person was simply not capable of performing the task; perhaps your briefing and training were inadequate; perhaps you were reluctant to hand over enough responsibility to enable the person to get the job done; perhaps you gave the person too much responsibility all at once without giving them enough support.

Listening to people

During your work as a manager, you are going to have to spend time listening to other people – listening to their problems, successes and worries, their reports on progress, their reasons for not progressing, their grievances and ideas. To do this effectively involves particular listening skills – often known as 'active listening' – which helps the other person gain a clearer understanding of the situation and to take responsibility for it.

Active listening describes the skill well since it is not passively absorbing what is being said but actively trying to understand what the speaker is saying and helping them to clarify it for both of you. It is one of the major skills of counselling, which we will be discussing in the next section and in Chapter 8. Active listening involves understanding the other person's view − getting 'inside' the speaker and suspending your own judgement. It is taking part in a two-way communication and it means letting the other person feel free to say whatever he or she wants or needs to say. This may mean you hear negative things about yourself in the process − you need to be prepared for this and must not jump in with some defensive statement.

The skills involved in active listening take time to acquire and need a lot of practice. As a manager, you have many opportunities for practice. Next time someone comes into your office with a problem, try the following:

- Either give them your full attention at that moment or arrange a time when you can give them all your attention.
- Don't take the words at face value; encourage the person to expand on what they are saying.
- Watch the non-verbal communication; is the person more or less worried than he or she appears − are there signs outside the words themselves which indicate anything?
- Check your understanding of what is being said; reflect in your own words what the speaker seems to be saying − perhaps you have misunderstood them.
- Try to convey 'I respect you as a person and feel you are worth listening to' through all your words and actions.

In your present job, you may feel more concerned with processes, products or services than with people. As you move up the organization, however, you become further removed from these and more involved in managing the people who are responsible for these processes, products or services. Listening to people will not only earn you their respect but it will help you to manage people more effectively.

Counselling

> 'Somebody called it "corridor conversations" − a slight exaggeration, but it does underline the fact that a lot of good counselling and helping is done in passing, does not need to take long, does not have to be in a formal setting and does not require a degree to do it'. (Reddy, 1987)

Counselling is used rather loosely as a term when, often, it means 'advising'. Organizations use counselling in a variety of ways, for example, career counselling, redundancy counselling and the kinds of counselling associated with appraisal systems and disciplinary procedures. It is used, mainly, to help employees solve their own problems or make their own decisions. Problems that need professional help, such as alcohol or drug abuse and serious marital or other domestic problems, should be referred to a specialist who is trained to give advice and help in these and other matters. Many companies are recognizing the benefits of employee counselling programmes, where external counsellors are made available to help employees.

Reddy, who has considerable experience of training and supervising counsellors, considers that effective counsellors need to be tolerant, have knowledge of themselves, be discreet and have an interest in and a liking for people (Reddy, 1987). Too often, people responsible for formal or informal counselling at work have no training and are lacking in some or all of the above qualities; they 'counsel' because it is part of their job.

It is often during the annual appraisal or performance review that counselling becomes a major part of the manager's job, particularly if you have to appraise someone who has been performing badly. This is the time when you have to get to the heart of what is causing inadequate performance – and the person being appraised may be reluctant to tell you or be unaware of the cause themselves.

The first essential is to define the problem between yourself and the other person and ensure that you both understand what it is. This involves the skills of 'active listening' we discussed earlier. For example, an employee who is not performing up to standard tells you emphatically that it is the fault of the new machine, the new process or a new member of staff – the 'it's not my fault' syndrome. By careful and sensitive probing, you discover that the fault lies in lack of training or the employee's fear that someone else will take over their job. The next stage in counselling is to get the employee to recognize this while you both accept that it is not necessarily 'their fault'.

Once the problem has been redefined in a way which satisfies you both – and this is not always possible – you need to be able to provide a solution which is mutually acceptable. This might involve offering training or support of some kind; it might involve ensuring that the person receives regular feedback on their performance, which reassures them that they are doing the job well or indicates ways in which they might improve their performance.

Throughout all this, you need to gain the trust of the other person. He or she needs to be sure that you have their interests at heart and that you are not likely to use the information you now have about them to their detriment. As a manager, you represent the organization when you are counselling subordinates; sometimes, the organization is at fault, by not providing adequate training, for example, or by decreasing an individual's job satisfaction. You, and the organization have then to take responsibility for contributing to the individual's problem.

INVESTIGATE

● *In what ways does your organization expect you to formally counsel your staff? Does it provide adequate resources (e.g. training) for this purpose and does it accept responsibility for contributing to problems when this occurs?*

Equal opportunities

> Complaints to the Equal Opportunities Commission about workplace discrimination increased by 40 per cent in 1991; enquiries about equal pay rose by 20 per cent and cases of sexual harassment increased by 30 per cent over the previous year.

Issues of equal opportunities for men and women, and policies of non-discrimination against employees (or potential employees in the case of recruitment and selection) on the grounds of gender, race or creed, are ones which every organization needs to address. Areas where discrimination occurs most frequently are those involved with pay, terms and conditions of employment, selection, promotion, transfers, training opportunities, benefits and redundancy. Failure to consider equal opportunity issues is not only morally unacceptable but can contravene the law and have expensive consequences for employers.

> Two nurses who were dismissed from the armed services after becoming pregnant were awarded compensation amounting to £25,000.

> Industrial tribunals have more than doubled the amount of compensation made for injury to feelings in discrimination cases between 1988 and 1991. Awards in cases of race discrimination are generally higher than those made in sex discrimination cases.

A formal investigation by the Commission for Racial Equality over the rejection of an Asian applicant for the post of principal at a further education college concluded that this was a case of direct racial discrimination.

The Fair Employment tribunal in Northern Ireland awarded a Catholic woman £25,000 in compensation after she had been refused a post by the Eastern Health and Social Services Board for unlawful discrimination on the grounds of religion.

A man who was made redundant chose to draw his pension at the age of 60. The company operated a pension scheme whereby women retired at 60 and men at 65. As a result, he only received two-thirds of what he would have received had he been a woman of the same age. His case was upheld by an industrial tribunal and the appeal has now been referred to the European Court of Justice.

The theme of equal opportunities, introduced in Chapters 2 and 3 in the context of recruitment and selection of staff, recurs constantly throughout this book. Not only is it raised in connection with gender, race and creed, but with respect to people with disabilities, people with fragmented career patterns, ex-offenders and older employees.

An Institute of Manpower Studies survey of 2,000 companies in 1991 found that only a minority were considering positive, long-term policies to attract older workers. (IMS, 'Last in the queue', 1992)

Responsibility for designing an equal opportunities policy lies with senior management: responsibility for implementing it lies with all managers. Any policy should provide for training of line managers and supervisors so that they understand the legal position and the organization's policy on equal opportunities. It should also provide for continuous monitoring and review of existing procedures and criteria to ensure that the policy is working in practice.

By law, organizations can undertake positive action not only to encourage the employment of people from minority groups but also to provide special training for them if they are under-represented in the workforce as a whole.

INVESTIGATE

- *Does your organization have an equal opportunities policy? Does it conform to this in practice? Can you identify areas within your sphere of responsibility where opportunities could be more 'equal' than they are at present?*

Managing conflict

Managing conflict is not the same as managing differences. Differences are inevitable in organizations: from time to time the interests of individuals and groups within the organization will diverge from organizational structures and goals. When 'differences' degenerate into conflict between individuals and groups, your job as a manager becomes more difficult.

Prior to her annual appraisal, Hamida was expecting praise for the number of lucrative contracts she had brought into the company. She was responsible to the production director for designing computer systems for hospital services and, over the past year, had been very successful in having these adopted, thus keeping the factory busy. However, her appraiser, who was the financial director, also gave her responsibility for making certain key returns, including the use of computer time. Instead of the praise she expected, she was reprimanded for being behind with the paperwork and threatened with downgrading if her handling of this did not improve. Hamida was deeply hurt since the reason she was behind with the returns was because she had insufficient clerical help; she become depressed and showed little interest in her work while telling everyone how unfairly she had been treated. It took a meeting between the production director, the financial director, Hamida and the staff trade union representative to sort out the situation.

This kind of conflict need never have arisen if the financial director had bothered to get a report on Hamida's performance from the production director and had taken any notice of her frequent requests for additional clerical assistance.

It would be ideal if we could always anticipate destructive conflict and ensure it was avoided. There are some generally recognized causes, although the extent to which conflict could be avoided in such situations is problematic. These include:

- **Grouping of activities within the organization** – conflict is likely to arise when one or other department or section becomes dependent on another which has different organizational goals. The example given earlier in this chapter about the different viewpoints of sales, finance and production staff highlights the potential for conflict.
- **Scarce resources** – when a number of departments or individuals are competing for the same limited resources such as staff or money.
- **Organizational politics** – where individuals or groups use power to control resources, influence organizational policy in their favour or protect traditional working practices in a time of change.
- **Unclear job responsibilities** – when individuals both consider the same part of a job to be their responsibility because job descriptions and role/responsibilities are not defined clearly.
- **Interpersonal** – which may be non-work based but bureaucratic and which can arise from personality clashes and similarities between people.

INVESTIGATE

- *Using the headings above, can you identify any current problems in your organization which could degenerate into open conflict between individuals or groups of people?*

As a manager, you can aim to prevent conflict erupting by creating an atmosphere in which collaboration between individuals is valued and interpersonal differences are accepted but are not allowed to jeopardize cooperation. This means allowing the freedom for individuals to express their feelings of dissatisfaction in a non-threatening atmosphere and for others to be willing to accept that differences of opinion exist. You also need to be aware of organizational politics – another 'fact' of working life – and individual needs for status, recognition and advancement. You also need to be seen to be scrupulously fair in allocating resources, consulting with those involved and being open about decisions. Shrugging your shoulders and saying 'It's not my fault – honest. It's the organization which makes all the decisions', is no help to anyone. As a manager, you have to fight your department's battles in the open.

If overt conflict develops, what can you do? You can try to ignore it in the hope that it will be resolved by someone else or go away of its own accord, or you might try to talk the people concerned out of making the problem so serious. You could even try to offer some alternative to one side or the other so that the conflict subsides, or even take one side against the other. Such strategies rarely work except in the short term.

Better practice is to try to bring the opposing parties together in an attempt to reconcile differences or, if that fails, to take the dispute to some higher and unbiased authority within the organization or outside it, such as the Advisory Conciliation and Arbitration Service (ACAS). Any solution is bound to be seen as a compromise, but at least it will be seen to be a fair compromise if it is clearly objective. This subject will be developed further in Chapter 8.

Health and safety at work

All employing organizations are governed by the Health and Safety at Work Act 1974 and a number of other acts which ensure that employees (and visitors) are protected as far as possible from accidental injury or illness caused by working conditions. These are summarized in the next section and new initiatives are likely under the Social Charter and European Community legislation. You do not need to be familiar with all the requirements of all the legislation unless you work in a Personnel Department, but the broad recommendations are valuable for everyone.

Legal and regulatory framework

Both the Equal Opportunities Commission and the Commission for Racial Equality provide Codes of Practice which offer guidance for employers and managers on equal opportunities in the workplace, and the Institute of Personnel Management have published 'The IPM Equal Opportunities Code'. The Employment Service has published a 'Code of Good Practice on the Employment of Disabled People' and the Institute of Personnel Management offer an employer's guide entitled 'Getting on with disabilities'.

The relevant Acts which set out the legal requirements of employers in the area of equal opportunities are:

- The Sex Discrimination Act 1975 (as amended by the Sex Discrimination Act 1986).
- The Race Relations Act 1976.
- The Disabled Persons (Employment) Act 1944.
- The Companies (Directors Report, Employment of Disabled Persons) Regulations 1980.

- The Rehabilitation of Offenders Act 1974.
- The Employment Protection Act 1975.
- The Employment Protection (Consolidation) Act 1978.
- The Health and Safety at Work Act 1974.

The main provisions of the Health and Safety at Work Act are:

- to secure the health, safety and welfare of people at work;
- to protect others from risks arising from the activities of people at work;
- to control the use and storage of dangerous substances;
- to control the emission into the atmosphere of noxious or offensive substances.

As an employer, it is necessary to provide:

- a safe place of work;
- a safe means of access to the place of work;
- a safe system of work;
- adequate materials;
- competent fellow employees;
- protection from unnecessary risk of injury;
- a safety policy;
- adequate instruction and training;
- a safety committee if union appointed safety representatives ask for one.

While at work, employees have a duty to take reasonable care of their own health and safety at work and of other persons who may be affected by their acts or omissions and cooperate with their employer or any other person in ensuring that the requirements are complied with.

Copies of regulations from the Health and Safety Executive and Health and Safety Commission are available from Her Majesty's Stationery Office.

The Health and Safety Executive (HSE) have also published a guide called 'Human factors in industrial safety' which looks at the roles of organizations, jobs and individuals in industrial safety and their practical control.

Not currently covered by the various Acts, but of concern to many employees, are problems associated with violence in the workplace, smoking at work and HIV/AIDS. The HSE provides a booklet on 'Preventing violence to staff' and the Institute of Personnel Management a guide on 'Smoking at work'. The Department of Employment and the Central Information Office issue guidelines on the risk of infection by HIV/AIDS.

Summary

In this chapter we have looked at your relations as a manager with individuals in the organization. The word 'individual' is important since it signals the differences in behaviour, ability and experience of those who work with, and for, you. It also indicates that different people will value different rewards from the work they do.

The work of Maslow, Herzberg and Moss Kanter helps us to understand the disparate needs that individuals have and what benefits they value in terms of job satisfaction and motivation to work. Herzberg also identifies factors which lead to below-average performance and suggests that the removal or improvement of these factors will reduce dissatisfaction. The particular role of pay in increasing or decreasing motivation is considered since it is the most common variant open to organizations and managers. In fact, the level of pay is not seen as having motivational impact but can be a source of dissatisfaction.

In his or her dealings with other people, a manager needs to delegate effectively and to be able to listen to and counsel staff with confidence and sensitivity. There are issues of equal opportunities, governed by law, which, if not recognized, can result in legal action by an employee who suffers discrimination. Managers need to be aware of equal opportunity policies within their organization and, even if these do not exist, the legal position regarding equality of pay and other work-related opportunities. He or she also needs to be able to recognize and cope with the signs and results of inter-personal differences which may deteriorate into destructive conflict. Objectivity and perceived fair play are the keynotes here.

Activities

1

How could you increase the motivation of your staff? Can you:
(a) Increase job 'satisfiers'?
(b) Decrease 'dissatisfiers'?

2

Many managers have problems with managing their time. One solution is to delegate effectively. How could you reduce your workload by delegating some of it to your subordinates and increase their job satisfaction at the same time?

3 List the number of times you are required to counsel staff on a formal or informal basis every week. How could you improve your counselling skills?

4 In what ways could you avert or reduce interpersonal conflict amongst your staff?

5 How familiar are you and your staff with the requirements of the Health and Safety at Work Act as it applies to your workplace? How could you improve their knowledge of the Act's requirements as these apply to their jobs?

References

Herzberg, F., Mausner, B. and Snyderman, B. B. (1959) *The Motivation to Work*, John Wiley, New York

Hunt, J. W. (1979) *Managing People at Work*, McGraw-Hill, Maidenhead

McGregor, D. (1960) *The Human Side of Enterprise*, McGraw-Hill, London

Maslow, A. H. (1943) A theory of human motivation. *Psychological Review*, **50**

Moss Kanter, R. (1977) *Men and Women of the Corporation*, Basic Books, New York

Reddy, M. (1987) *The Manager's Guide to Counselling at Work*, British Psychological Society/Methuen, London

Taylor, F. W. (1947) *Scientific Management*, Harper and Row, New York

Wrightsman, L. S. (1974) *Assumptions about Human Nature*, Brooks/Cole, Monterey, Ca

Further reading

Egan, G. (1962) *The Skilled Helper*, Brooks/Cole, Monterey, Ca

Pugh, D. S. and Hickson, D. J. (1989) *Writers on Organisations*, Penguin, Harmondsworth (summarizes many of the essential theories of motivation)

Reddy, M. (1987) *The Manager's Guide to Counselling*, British Psychological Society/Methuen, London

Sneider, R. and Ross, R. (1992) *From Equality to Diversity: a Business Case for Equal Opportunities*, Pitman, London

5 Managing people in groups

Introduction

Having accepted that there is a range of reasons why people behave differently in a work situation and that you cannot make wild and generalized assumptions about any individual's reasons for performing better or worse than average, you will recognize that when you put individuals together into a group, the behaviour of that group is likely to be unpredictable. Managers spend up to 80 per cent of their time in meetings, many of which constitute working groups, so it is important that they understand about the behaviour of groups.

In this chapter, we will be examining:

- How people behave in groups.
- The purposes of work groups.
- Informal groups at work.
- The stages of group formation.
- Group dynamics.
- What makes work groups perform effectively.

This theme of working in groups will be continued in Chapter 6 when we look at building and leading teams.

Management in practice

People's behaviour in groups

In most organizations, people work in groups at some time or another – in committees, in project teams, or on working parties. In some cases, work is always undertaken by small groups and people rarely work on their own; in other words, the task determines the working practice. This is usually because the task is relatively complex and requires the combined abilities of a number of people or because it involves cooperation between a number of individuals. Organizations themselves tend to be run by small senior management teams today rather than by large boards or by individuals. This is partly because large groups are not as effective at responsive decision-making as smaller ones of around five to seven members and partly because organizations are faced with a massive amount of complex decision-making. There is also a tendency to believe that power in organizations should be shared rather than being in the hands of one person. However, the prevalent practice of working in small groups is not always entirely successful.

In common with many organizations, Shell UK adopted a policy of decentralizing its decision-making in the late 1980s, giving more responsibility to small groups in its business units. As a consequence, the company found that communication suffered and the units became cut off from each other and from the expertise at the centre: the quality of decision-making suffered, resulting in over-runs on some major projects and a deterioration in operational reliability. The company is now reconsidering its policy.

A strong group is also usually more powerful than a sole individual and can have a considerable effect on organizational policy and practice. This can be seen in the political arena where pressure groups can affect government policy − for example, environmental pressure groups have had a strong effect on the government's attitude towards pollution and health. In the case of a management buy-out by a group of employees, organizations have often taken on a fresh life and become much more successful than before.

A great deal of psychological research has been undertaken on the way people's behaviour changes when they become part of a group. There is, for example, a great pressure for people to conform to the accepted behaviour of the group − known as 'group norms'. Permanent work groups, where membership only changes when someone leaves the group or a new member enters it, develop norms over a long period which become quite rigid; temporary work groups, however, will not develop such stringent norms.

Group norms include the kind of behaviour which is acceptable to the members of the group, such as the degree of formality of its meetings, the way it divides up its work, the leadership style adopted and so on. At the level of detail, group norms can include the way people dress, how they use equipment, attitudes to safety regulations, where each person sits, when rest periods are taken etc. As long as all its members conform to these unwritten 'rules', the group will be a close-knit entity which resists change to its working practices, although this does not necessarily mean it is particularly effective. Group members who do not conform are regarded with suspicion and pressure is put on them by others to modify their behaviour so that they 'fit in'.

When Mike was invited to join the Computer Implementation Group he was delighted that he would now have the opportunity to influence the company's policy on computerizing its systems. He spoke eloquently and at length on his vision for the future at his first meeting and was satisfied that he had made a number of important points. However, when he read the minutes of the meeting, he saw that this contribution had been relegated to a few lines whereas the main business appeared to have been the siting of the new mainframe, even though this had been agreed months earlier.

He confided his bewilderment to another member of the group who said 'But that's the way things happen here. What you said was interesting — although you took far too long about it; no one ever speaks for more than a few minutes at these meetings. You're very new to all this. Wait a bit before you come in with all these new ideas and then only one at a time.'

Mike would not believe him and tried again; he was politely ignored by the other members who were trying to get to grips with some system for improving internal mail sorting. Eventually, he took the other person's advice and kept quiet for a few months. When he eventually put forward his idea for changing the program the company used for its annual budgeting exercise, he was taken more seriously — he had 'conformed' and the group was prepared, at least, to listen to what he had to say.

There are trade-offs in being a member of a group. You may have to conform to behaviour which, as an individual, you are not used to or find difficult. However, your acceptance by such a group will depend on the extent to which you conform to its norms. If you do conform, you will be accepted as a group member and share fully in its activities.

Groups often rely on consensus in making decisions. Not everyone may agree individually on which way the decision should go, but will agree with the majority. Consensus decision-making is usually effective in that all the individual members of the group have had a chance to air their views and to listen to the views of colleagues; if the eventual decision is agreed by the majority and the minority accept it, it is usually sound. Unless, of course, the group has reached the stage of 'groupthink'.

The phenomenon of 'groupthink', identified by Janis (1982), tends to occur when a group has been formed for some considerable time, there is strong group pressure and there is over-confidence by its members in the group's power and influence. There is a marked deterioration in the group's efficiency and it tends to believe in its own morality — it thinks it is indispensable and invincible, and always right. As a result, it considers any decision it makes, good or bad, will be the correct one and gives up evaluating the quality of the decisions it makes. This can become a very dangerous situation if the group is powerful.

The purposes of work groups

Organizations create formal work groups for a number of reasons. Charles Handy (1990) identifies the following:

- for the distribution of work;
- for the management and control of work;
- for problem-solving and decision-making;
- for processing information;
- for testing and ratifying decisions;
- for coordination and liaison;
- for increasing commitment and involvement;
- for negotiation and conflict resolution;
- for inquest or enquiry into the past.

INVESTIGATE

- *Think of any work group of which you are a member and, from the above list, try to identify its purpose(s).*

Sometimes, groups try to fulfil more than one function or overflow from one function to another. For example, if a group has been successful in problem-solving and decision-making, it might be asked to carry out the tasks of negotiation and conflict resolution associated with the decisions it has reached. However, this may be short-sighted. The same group may not be so successful in its second purpose simply because it was successful in its first.

The kinds of groups which carry out the functions suggested by Handy are nearly always formally created and constituted by the organization. In this way, they have organizational authority to perform their stated function (but not, necessarily, to carry out other associated functions). Informal or interest groups also exist in organizations as you will see in the next section.

People belong to groups for a number of reasons. One reason for belonging to a group is the satisfaction of what Maslow defined as 'social needs' and, indeed, what Herzberg identified as a desire to be recognized (see Chapter 4); people can define their identity through their membership of certain groups. People belong to local political or pressure groups, for example, because they experience a shared set of values with the other people in the group which reinforces their own values.

At work, however, they may be asked, or told, to join a certain work group because of particular knowledge or experience in some area which is necessary to the group's performance; they may represent some staff category or other organizational purpose; they may have certain power within the organization and be able to get things done. Their original purpose for being in the group may have nothing to do with their social needs and they may feel alienated amongst people whose values are different from their own and in line with the particular norms of the group. The group, however, must have a shared purpose, which needs to be clearly identified if the organization expects everyone in it to work towards the same objectives.

> Safeway, the retail foodstore chain, has a clear mission statement which is included in each member of staff's job description. It permeates the company and work groups are clear that whatever they are asked to do, or choose to do, must fulfil the same purpose.

INVESTIGATE

• *Think of any formal work group of which you are a member. Does it have clear objectives which are understood and shared by all its members? How do these objectives relate to the overall objective or mission statement of your organization?*

Informal groups at work

Organizations also breed informal groups which spring up despite, and sometimes in opposition to, the organization. These may be formed by people who share a common problem at work or dissatisfaction with working conditions. For this reason they are often referred to as 'interest' groups since the members of the group share a common interest in work-related matters. They may be formed through some shared concern such as a desire for equal opportunities practices at work or the perceived need for a staff canteen or a non-smoking policy. Or they may be groups of people with shared interests and beliefs outside their work context – for example in voluntary work, amateur dramatics or a particular religion. These groups have no authority in the eyes of the organization, although they can satisfy social needs and may create considerable pressure for change.

The kinds of issues which give rise to the formation of interest groups include the following, identified by Professor Sandra Dawson of Imperial College, London (Dawson, 1992):

- The division of organizational profit between different groups associated with the organization.
- How pay increases or promotion are secured.
- How to avoid redundancy and gain job security.
- How people are treated by their bosses.
- What is a 'good' job.
- How different functions in the organization should link together and what is their relative importance.
- The amount of 'discretion' or 'control' over different jobs.
- The way the organization should be going.

These are the kinds of issues which can be the subject of conversation amongst employees over lunch or during a coffee break — the core of 'corridor conversations'. Often, the people who take part in them do not see themselves as a member of an informal or interest group — they see the issues as matters of common concern. Yet, not always does everyone share this concern; in some cases, one person may sympathize with another over a particular issue but have no personal interest in it themselves. As you will see in Chapter 8, a group of people who share a common grievance can make more impact than a single individual.

A college was attempting to change its organizational structure. Currently, it was run by the Principal and two Deputy Principals with other staff taking on informal roles in staff development, curriculum and course design and student counselling. It was generally agreed that the Principal's role was too demanding of a single person and that the roles of the Deputy Principals were unclear and ill-defined. It was also recognized by some staff that the changes in higher education meant an increase in competitiveness and a need for some overt marketing which would increase and change the roles of the existing senior staff.

A small group was set up to look at reorganizing the structure of the college, consisting of a number of people who had expressed considerable interest in this. They followed all the 'rules' for group effectiveness, particularly in communicating their discussions to everyone else. Yet they were disappointed that many of the staff showed little interest in what was going on; they were reasonably happy with the existing structure and either saw no reason to change it or said they would accept any changes that were proposed.

At the same time, the secretarial staff of the college were involved in re-defining their jobs. No formal grouping was set up, yet every member of secretarial and clerical staff took a deep interest in what was going on.

Interest groups may become semi-formalized, as in the first group in the example above, or they may have no real grouping, not even on an informal basis. In some cases, they may exist because people in organizations have professional knowledge and values in common, such as men and women who have trained as engineers or as personnel specialists. These individuals have already shared in a specific and lengthy training, with restricted entry and a commitment to a distinct body of specialized knowledge which gives them a shared interest (Dawson, 1992).

INVESTIGATE

- *Do any interest groups exist in your organization? Are they semi-formal, informal or unformed?*

Stages in the development of groups

Before a group can perform effectively, it needs to go through a number of stages. Four of these were identified by Tuckman (1965) as:

- Forming
- Storming
- Norming
- Performing

To these, we could add a fifth stage:

- Mourning

Forming

This is the initial, testing stage when the group comes together for the first few meetings. At this stage, the group is merely a collection of individuals, each with personal ideas and agendas, wanting to see how they will 'fit in' and what the other members of the group are like.

Typical behaviour at this point will be wary; individuals will be polite to each other and somewhat guarded in what they say or agree to do. They will probably not divulge anything about themselves unless asked to do so. They will be assessing the group leader – is he or she likely to be formal or informal, directive or consultative? What kind of authority has the leader got? There will be a considerable amount of silence as people weigh each other up and most of the discussion will probably be concerned with structure — what the group is going to do, how work will be divided up, what are the objectives of the task.

One way of helping to reduce anxiety at this stage is for the group to undergo some kind of 'icebreaking' exercise. This could take the form of each person interviewing another and then 'introducing' that person to the rest of the group. Certainly, namecards are helpful at this stage when people often do not know the names of the other members of the group.

Storming

The second stage of group formation is characterized by conflict, which may be open or hidden. Although, in the initial stage, agreement may appear to have been reached about group objectives, leadership, roles etc., these may be challenged in the second stage. Individual members may start to test their strength. This may take the form of outright confrontation such as 'What right do you have to say that?' or 'I didn't agree with her ideas at the time and I still don't.' Or people may simply opt out and refuse to take part in discussion or work with other people. Sub-groups are likely to form — there is strength in alliances and people often feel happier if they can share their feelings and grievances with other sympathetic members of the group.

The group can feel it is not getting anywhere during this storming phase, which is depressing for its members, and it can even degenerate into a noisy and rebellious band of squabbling and in-fighting individuals. This, however, is the worst scenario and most people realize that it is unproductive. It is usually better for the leader of the group — or one or more of its members — to bring the conflict out into the open and try to discuss it. In reality, this often means going back to the first stage and re-defining the objectives and roles of the group. If this is successful, members of the group will develop trust in each other which is essential to the group's working successfully.

Norming

At this stage, once the group is clear about what it is going to do and has passed through the earlier stages, it can begin to get itself organized. By this time, clearer roles are emerging and people are more certain about what they are expected to contribute. This is when the group begins to establish procedures and group norms and when individuals test the working of the group and determine their levels of commitment to it.

It is a period when, providing trust has been established, people can confront issues and give constructive feedback to each other.

People will begin to talk more openly and learn to listen to the views of others. Even when these views conflict with their own, they will be prepared to give them serious consideration. The group is moving towards solidarity.

Performing

This stage will only be reached when the other three stages have been completed successfully; some groups never reach it. The individual members of the group will have established rapport with others, making allowances for weaknesses and building on individual and group strengths. There will be both an open atmosphere in which problems and ideas can be talked about and resolved without conflict and a close, supportive ambience with which individuals feel comfortable − a sense of 'belonging'. By the time the group reaches this stage, it is at its most productive.

Mourning

The word 'mourning' denotes the breaking up of a successful group − group members 'mourn' the loss of the support and group identity they had valued. However, it should also be a time of remembering what went on in the group and what made it so successful − a period of evaluation from which everyone can learn something about being a group member. Too often, the memory of a highly successful group acquires a kind of aura which clouds the recollection of its less successful functioning − particularly of the 'storming' phase. Ideally, everyone needs to learn from each experience of working in a group so that they can increase their personal effectiveness as a group member.

Not all stages will take the same length of time. For a group whose members already know each other and where the task is relatively simple and highly defined, such as 'Produce an outline induction and training programme for new staff in the Department', the first three stages may be dealt with in a few hours. For a more complex task, with low definition and where people are coming together in a group for the first time (such as in a project team), you should expect the stages to take considerably longer.

Group dynamics

Organizations which run training courses for managers and others outside the organization are able to introduce the idea of group dynamics in a realistic way. For a period of time, usually about a week, people from different organizations and working backgrounds are thrown together to work intensively in small groups, analysing and solving problems and reaching decisions. Part of this time is often spent in reflecting on the way in which the group is behaving – the *process* of group dynamics rather than the *content* of the task it has been set.

This may sound like contemplation of one's own navel, but it is usually a very rewarding aspect of these kinds of training courses. It has to be handled sensitively, of course, since people are likely to discover things about themselves which they would rather not know. However, this is not so threatening in a situation where they will not be working with the others in this group again, or even in the same organization.

The previous section outlined the stages a group goes through when it takes on a task. This can be used as the basis for looking at how the group is behaving at any time during its formation. Group dynamics, however, also focuses on the individual – how he or she is behaving, how he or she relates to other members of the group, what any person is contributing, whether individuals are seeking power or are opting out or whether some group members are being deliberately or unwittingly excluded. The essential ingredient for examining group dynamics is trust between its members so that anyone can speak openly about their feelings and reactions.

The task the group is undertaking usually assumes prime importance, particularly when groups are competing with each other on the same task as happens on training courses. It happens in organizations too, when different project teams are competing for additional resources or individuals are seeking rewards. In particular, ambitious and confident people can run away with the task without realizing that what they are doing is not necessarily the only, or best way of tackling it. Since they do not listen to others in the group, they are not using the potential resources which a group of people brings to any problem.

Sue was a very high-powered Chief Executive in her real-life role and expected to adopt the leadership of any group she worked in. However, working with other senior people outside her organization, she discovered that she was in competition for leadership of the group. At first she tried to assert herself by being aggressive and, when that failed, decided she would have nothing further to do with the group. During discussions, she had to come to terms with the fact that she was a fairly large fish in a rather small pond in her own organization and lacked some essential leadership skills.

Sam was a member of a group of twelve people, working on a problem-solving exercise. He felt his ideas were ignored and that nobody listened to him. He confided in the group leader that he suspected racial discrimination since everyone else in the group was white. At a group meeting, he discovered that three other people felt exactly the same way as he did, in that they also felt excluded, and it was agreed that the group was too large to function effectively and that it would work as two sub-groups in future. Sam agreed that the problem was one of size rather than of colour or race.

Group effectiveness

There are a large number of factors which interact to determine how effective − or ineffective − a group may be. These include:

- The size of the group.
- The characteristics of its members.
- The stages of its development.
- The task the group has to undertake.
- The kind of organization in which the group is working.
- The group leader.
- Group processes and procedures.
- Group communication.

With the exception of the stages a group passes through, which were covered earlier, we will look at each of these in turn.

Group size

The optimum size of a work group is between five and seven members. This size of group allows everyone to participate more or less equally and to get to know each other reasonably well. Once the group becomes larger, participation and communication become more problematic.

Yet some groups need to be larger because the task requires a number of specialists or because widespread representation is thought to be essential. In these cases, it is usually better to divide the group into sub-groups, each with its own responsibilities, meeting as a large group only when it is necessary. Committees, for example, which are often too large because of the need for representation from a number of different parts of the organization, usually operate more effectively when Working Parties or Task Forces are formed from amongst the members for specific tasks. Groups with over twenty members which do not break down into sub-groups tend to suffer from absenteeism and low morale.

Group member characteristics

Although people who think and act in similar ways may feel happier working in a group together, this is not always a recipe for success. A mix of skills and characteristics is necessary for a group to be effective. In the next chapter, we will be looking at the kinds of roles people can adopt in groups and how the mix of roles contributes to the group's success. At this stage, however, it is important to recognize that many groups are determined by the individual's role in the organization – manager, charge-hand, union representative and so on. Although these hierarchical roles may determine who belongs to a particular work group, the individual's role in that group may not be the same as the title he or she possesses in organizational terms.

The task

People are brought together into work groups because there is a particular task which the organization has identified as needing to be undertaken. These tasks relate back to Handy's purposes of work groups and might include problem-solving, idea generation, planning and implementing change, quality improvement, decision-making, policy formation, procedural definition etc. The type of task will determine who belongs to the group. For example, how many and which specialists or experts are needed, which parts of the organization need to be represented.

The timescale of the task is also an important factor. If the job needs to be completed urgently, a highly structured group with an authoritative leader may be acceptable. Where there is less pressure of time and creative ideas are sought, this is likely to be less acceptable.

The organization

Organizations have their own norms about the way in which things are done and this will be reflected in their work groups. A very bureaucratic organization, for example, such as the Civil Service or the Army, will have procedures for almost any task that needs a work group, even down to who should be members of certain groups. In such circumstances the position of the group leader in the organization's hierarchy is likely to be unchallenged in the work group.

The group leader

As you will have realized, the person who is responsible for leading any group is likely to contribute considerably to the group's success or failure. In some organizations, as we have pointed out, the group leader will have the authority of his or her position in that organization's hierarchy. In other, less highly structured organizations, the leader may lack any recognizable organizational power but may lead the group because they have particular expertise or knowledge which other members of the group lack. Another reason for the choice of a particular person as leader is that they are responsible for and control the group's budget − in this case, 'money is power'. However, even when a formal leader has been appointed from outside or from within the group in its initial 'forming' stage', other people may assume this role. If the leader is poor, unable to encourage the group to get on with its task or to deal with conflict between individual group members, the group is not likely to be very effective. Another person may take over the leadership or this role may be shared by a number of people depending on the task. For example, someone who is knowledgeable about budgeting could assume leadership when decisions need to be made about costing or expenditure; someone else, with a knowledge of personnel procedures, might take on the role where matters relating to staff recruitment, deployment or downsizing are concerned.

Processes and procedures

These refer to the way in which the group conducts itself in performing its tasks and looking after its members. One model of group process which is effective in approaching a problem-solving task systematically involves going through six steps.

First, the problem needs to be identified and described, preferably as clearly as possible by the person who has recognized it. If it is a problem which the group has been asked to tackle from outside, it still needs to be defined by the group so that everyone understands exactly what it is. This involves the second step, seeking information which will clarify the group's understanding of the problem, often from outside the group. This leads to the third stage − diagnosis. The problem has been identified and all the necessary information about it has been acquired; now the group can effectively determine what the real problem is. Once the problem has been diagnosed, opinions can be put forward by individual group members (the fourth step) and these can be evaluated by other members (step five) before a decision (step six) is made. This kind of rational approach to solving problems and making decisions optimizes the contribution of all the members of the group.

Group communication

When people are working together in a group, the way in which they communicate with each other and with people outside the group affects the way in which the group performs.

Within the group, some pattern of communication usually emerges.

One individual may take on all the responsibility of communicating with each member of the group, letting everyone know what everyone else is doing, keeping records, collecting and disseminating information. This works well in a small group and means that everyone is aware of what is going on — provided the individual does the job well. An alternative pattern is where communication is passed on from one person to another. This is slow and often unreliable, as communication can be distorted.

A pattern of 'all-channel' communication inside the group is effective for complex problems whereby everyone is in constant communication with everyone else. Again, this works better in smaller groups since, as the size of the group increases, so does the complexity of this kind of communication. There is also a 'breakdown' factor if one or more group members do not communicate with others.

Communicating with others outside the group is often essential, particularly at a time of change. There is a tendency for groups to become very inward-focusing, forgetting about other people, other departments in the wider organization. These others often need to know, and usually want to know, what the group is doing and how it is progressing. This sort of communication may take place in formal reports to a person to whom the group is responsible, or it may take the form of a wider, public relations exercise through a newsletter to other staff.

The group also needs communication from outside; it needs to be aware of what is happening elsewhere in the organization which might affect its own task; it might need to know what other work groups are doing, particularly if their tasks overlap. No work group is an island and it will certainly not be effective if it believes it is.

Summary

In this chapter we have looked at how people behave when they are formed into work groups. Groups can either be formal, in which case they are constituted and recognized by the organization, or informal, in which case they are often not recognized.

Formal groups can have one or more work-related purposes and need to be clear about their objectives. All groups which meet for a particular purpose pass through a number of stages before they are able to perform effectively, although the length of these stages will vary depending on the membership of the group and the task it has been set.

There are a number of factors which affect how well a work group performs. These include the size of a group, its membership, the task(s) it has to perform, the norms of the organization, the way in which it goes about its work and the way in which it communicates between its members and to other people.

Activities

1

Make a list of groups in your organization about which you are aware. Note beside each one (a) its purpose and (b) whether it is formal, informal or an interest group.

2

Take a group of which you are an active member. What stage in its development has this group reached? Has it moved on or is it moving on through all four stages?

3

Using the headings in the last section, try to assess the effectiveness of your main work group and identify how it might become more effective.

References

Dawson, S. (1992) *Analysing Organizations*, 2nd edn, Macmillan, London
Handy, C. (1990) *Understanding Organisations*, Penguin, Harmondsworth
Janis, I. L. (1982) *Groupthink*, Houghton-Mifflin, Boston, Mass.
Tuckman, B. W. (1965) Development sequences in small groups. *Psychological Bulletin*, **63**

Further reading

Handy, C. (1990) *Understanding Organisations*, Penguin, Harmondsworth, Chapter 6
Homans, G. C. (1951) *The Human Group*, Routledge and Kegan Paul, London
Zander, A. (1983) *Making Groups Effective*, Jossey-Bass, San Francisco, Ca.

6 Building your team

Introduction

Following on from what you have learned about the ways people behave in groups, and how groups can be more, or less, effective, this chapter concentrates on the development and improvement of teams.

Although you may have inherited existing teams in your work, or become a member of an existing team yourself, you are likely to become involved in setting up work teams at some time or another. To do this, you will need to identify the skill or competence requirements needed in team members in relation to the demands of the task. Having done this, you need to identify and assess competences in potential team members in the same way as you needed to assess current skills in relation to recruitment and selection of new staff (Chapter 2).

Having selected the members of your team, you, as manager, need to establish and agree objectives for team development and working. This may involve using project planning and resource allocation techniques, the details of which are beyond the scope of this book. You will also need to define and allocate workload responsibilities and authority within the team and ensure that you give members of your team constructive feedback on their performance.

In order to maximize team performance, you will need to motivate your staff to reach the team's objectives (see Chapter 4) and provide for learning and skill development where necessary.

Managing a team involves establishing good relationships with all its members through genuine consultation and the establishment of clear lines of communication. This involves not only communicating 'outwards' to others — giving instructions, setting deadlines and so on — but being receptive to 'inward' communication from team members and others. Only by doing this can you assess information which is important and appropriate for your team to receive.

You are also likely to lead team meetings and some advice on that will be given here, although full coverage of that subject would require a book of its own.

In this chapter we will be looking at:

- Forming a team.
- Team roles.

- Leading a team.
- Setting objectives.
- Monitoring and evaluating progress.
- Running team meetings.
- Managing multicultural teams.
- The benefits of teams.

Management in practice

Forming a team

Mike Woodcock and Dave Francis, in their book *Organisation Development through Teambuilding* (1990), state that an effective team will show the following characteristics:

- It will establish and work towards clear objectives.
- It will have open relationships between members.
- It will deal with different viewpoints and gain from debate.
- Members will show a high level of support for each other.
- Personal relationships will be based on personal knowledge and trust.
- People will want to work together and get things done.
- Potentially damaging conflicts will be worked through and resolved.
- Procedures and decision-making processes will be effective.
- Leadership will be skilful and appropriate to the needs of the team.
- It will regularly review its operations and try to learn from experiences.
- Individuals will be developed and the team will be capable of dealing with strong and weak personalities.
- Relations with other groups will be cooperative and open.

Mike Woodcock (1989) identifies problems with ineffective teams, which may be due to:

- Poor selection and recruitment of team members.
- Confused organization structure.
- Lack of control of the team by the leader.
- Poor training of team members.
- Low motivation.
- Low creativity in team members.
- An inappropriate management philosophy.
- Lack of succession planning and development.
- Unclear aims.
- Unfair or inappropriate rewards.
- Personal stagnation in team members or leader.

INVESTIGATE

- *Think of a team of which you are either the leader or an active member. Using the above lists as a check, identify which characteristics of your team are present and how effective − or ineffective − it is.*

This, then, is what you should be aiming for when setting up and developing a team. Your job will be easier if you are able to select team members yourself based on the demands of the task and the skills and competences required to complete it.

In Chapter 2 on recruitment you were introduced to the idea of job descriptions and employee specifications. The same techniques can be used to identify what the team has to carry out and what kinds of people would be necessary in the team. However, as you will see in the next section, you also have to take into account the balance of people in your team and the kinds of characteristics possessed by individuals. Of course, this assumes an ideal situation in which you are free to choose who will be in your team and those you select are both able and willing to be in it. Organizational reality means that you often have to include certain people because of their work role or place in the hierarchy or that the people you want are already committed to other projects or work.

As leader of a new team, you have to analyse the task it is expected to perform and the skills you will need; to do this you will need a form of 'job description' which sets out the requirements of the task. For example, suppose you were asked to set up a team of people to assess different types of computer software and introduce the preferred option into your department or organization. You might draw up a description of the task in the following way:

Objective: To implement the most appropriate software programme into . . . . . . within a period of x months at no more than y cost [of course, your timescale and budget may not be determined at this stage.]

Method:
- identify current and forecast software needs of department/ organization
- identify appropriate commercial software packages
- test software packages
- consider design of package if no appropriate commercial package available
- select or design appropriate software
- load software on to hardware

— train staff in use of software
— evaluate implementation

This would only be a very rough, first shot at defining the team's task. Once the team is set up, you may have to redefine it in the light of more knowledge about what has to be done.

Looking at this rough description, it is obvious that you are going to need people with computing skills and, possibly, with the competence to design custom-made software. But you are also going to need people who can communicate what the team is doing to others outside the team. You will need to identify the current and future needs of people who will be using the new package. These people may be worried about their ability to operate it, particularly if it is very complex and/or specialized; they will need reassurance. You will also need people who are good trainers, not just people who are good operators. You will also need team members who are willing to undertake the rather unexciting work of testing the software packages ... and so on.

Your team member 'employee specification' grows by the minute and, from the last chapter, you know that large teams are less effective than small ones. Of course, you can always elect to work in sub-groups but you need to ensure that people who are going to be working together in small groups not only have the required competence but can work together. If possible, you want to reduce the risk of interpersonal conflict within the group.

One way of deciding upon who should join your team is to look at the team role that a person can play quite apart from his or her particular expertise. Belbin, whose work on management teams (1981, 1993) is well known, differentiates between functional roles such as computer analyst, sales manager, accountant and so on, and team roles which relate to an individual's contribution to the effectiveness of the team. By identifying the particular roles team members can play and by recognizing individual strengths and weaknesses in relation to these roles, you can build a well-balanced and effective team.

Team roles

Belbin investigated mixed management teams over a long period and concluded that any team member could play one or more of the following roles:

- Implementer
- Coordinator
- Shaper
- Plant

- Resource Investigator
- Monitor/Evaluator
- Teamworker
- Completer/Finisher
- Specialist

He devised a Self Perception Inventory which can be used by individual team members to determine in which roles they are strongest and in which they are weakest. (Find this Inventory in Belbin's book *Management Teams* (1991) and try it out for yourself.) Each role has positive and negative aspects which it is necessary for the individual and other team members to recognize.

Implementer

This person is disciplined, conscientious and aware of external responsibilities such as the need to keep other people informed about what the team is doing. He or she respects established conditions in the organization and one weakness of the role is a degree of rigidity. On the positive side, this person is very practical, trusting and tolerant of other people. The Implementer's strengths lie in putting other people's ideas and plans into operation and carrying out plans which the team have agreed in a systematic and efficient way.

Coordinator

As you might expect, this denotes the ability to lead the team towards its objectives through effective use of team members. The Coordinator is able to recognize individual strengths and weaknesses in other members of the team and ensure that the best use is made of every person's potential. This role has many positive aspects, its main weakness being that a Coordinator is not usually so effective at 'crisis' management; he or she is likely to prefer a participative, consultative style of leadership, carrying all the rest of the team with them. In cases where the team needs to act under pressure and at high speed, the Shaper can take over.

Shaper

Shapers are people who have a strong need for achievement and success. They are highly competitive with an active desire to win — they put life into a team and can drive through change at the expense of popularity. On the negative side, Shapers are often seen as pushy and aggressive and insensitive to the feelings of others.

The Coordinator and Shaper roles are complementary; the former pulls a team together while the latter challenges the status quo and goads other team members into action.

Plant

The Plant is the creative member of the team, full of new ideas and ways of doing things and particularly concerned with finding innovative solutions to major issues. They generally have higher than average intelligence. Often, however, they are weak in communicating their ideas to others and can appear to be on a different wavelength; they are also very sensitive to criticism or praise. If a team contains too many people who are strong in this role, they can conflict with each other over ideas.

The name derives from Belbin's experiments in which he 'planted' individuals who scored highly on creativity in psychometric tests into the companies he was studying (Belbin, 1981).

Resource Investigator

When studying managers who might be classified as 'Plants', Belbin identified another, complementary role − the Resource Investigator. More outgoing and communicative than the Plant, this person gets around, finds out what is going on, meets people and asks relevant questions. This person is often described as 'never being in the office and, if he or she is, always on the telephone'. Resource Investigators are good communicators and negotiators, always ready to explore new opportunities and make new contacts. They are also good at thinking on their feet and getting information. However, they can quickly lose enthusiasm if the task is not stimulating enough for them.

Monitor/Evaluator

Although both Plants and Resource Investigators are valued by teams for their ideas and enthusiasm respectively, both can get carried away if there is no Monitor/Evaluator present. This person is serious-minded and judicious, valued for an ability to make shrewd judgements and able to debate with a Plant over the latter's ideas. To other team members, the Monitor/Evaluator can appear as rather dry, boring and over-critical, but this role is essential in a team where the decision-making process is complicated and it is difficult to reach consensus; the Monitor/Evaluator can be relied upon to reach the optimum decision.

Teamworker

Teamworkers are diplomatic and perceptive with a strong interest in people. They are good at building on other people's suggestions, improving communications between different members of the team and generally fostering team spirit. They are particularly effective at averting interpersonal conflict and dealing with difficult team members. The Teamworker will let the Plants in the team have their say even if their ideas may appear impractical to others; he or she can draw out the slower but essential Monitor/Evaluator. A team composed of Teamworkers might sound ideal, but they lack the attributes of some of the other roles and members of such a team would spend all their time supporting one another!

Completer/Finisher

So far we have identified team members who represent the aims of the organization, who can lead the team during stable times and in periods of crisis, people who will have ideas, people who communicate well, people who can reach decisions and people who encourage cooperation; the Completer/Finisher is the final ingredient. He or she is the person who has the ability to carry anything through to its conclusion with complete thoroughness. A team may have many brilliant ideas and even reach decisions, but if the agreed action is not carried out, it will fail in its objectives. This person checks on every detail and ensures nothing is overlooked. Completer/Finishers have high standards for themselves and others and may often be intolerant of people who do not share these standards.

Specialist

This is the person with professional expertise in an area valued and needed by the team in order to achieve its objectives. A team may need more than one Specialist at different times in its evolution. For example, a team involved in a building project would need an architect at the design stage and perhaps someone with expertise in the different properties of particular building materials: they might also need expert help on costing, on computer trunking and so on.

Of course, these team roles are stereotypes and individuals are usually strong in one or two aspects and weak in others. The same person can, therefore, perform more than one role in a team; you do not have to have teams of nine people to fulfil all the roles. The important point is that teams which are well-balanced in terms of the roles team members play will be more effective than teams which are imbalanced and where one or more essential team roles are missing.

INVESTIGATE

- *Imagine that you could form your ideal team. Try to identify people in your organization who would be strong in each of the nine Belbin team roles.*

Unfortunately, in real life teams are not always well-balanced. What you should have learned from the discussion of team roles is the reason why some teams are more effective than others. You should be able to recognize the shortcomings in any team of which you are a member.

When you are setting up a team, it is useful to spend some time asking everyone to identify their own strengths and weaknesses and to discuss these with other team members. You could use Belbin's Self Perception Inventory as a starting point. As a result, as a team you will be aware of any general weakness, such as not having anyone whose strength lies in communicating with others or lacking any Plants and thus being short of creative ideas. If you work in a team most of the time, this should also give you some guidance about the kinds of people you need to recruit.

Leading a team

In the last section we identified two kinds of people who might assume leadership of a team — the Coordinator and the Shaper — depending on the kind of task which the team had been set. Team leadership is not always vested in the person who has been given that position by the organization. It may change hands depending on the situation. For example, there will be times when the team needs to be led by a specialist if it encounters technical or other specialized difficulties; at other times it may be led by someone who has had previous experience of a particular type of problem or project. The best teams profit from the strengths of individual members and recognize when 'leadership' should pass to the most appropriate person. However, someone usually has the responsibility and title of 'team leader', at least in the eyes of the organization, and is accountable for the team's performance.

There are almost as many theories about leaders and leadership as there are different kinds of people. Early research concentrated on trying to identify the personality characteristics of 'good' leaders — and failed. People who were considered to be successful leaders had different characteristics, different levels of intelligence, different skills. Later research looked at the way leaders behaved in different situations, but most experts in the field conclude that leadership cannot be explained just by studying individuals. The leader of a team needs to be related to the task which is being carried out, the needs of the team and the needs of individuals in that team. One useful way of looking at this is to use a simple diagram of interlocking circles (Figure 6.1).

As was pointed out earlier, the kind of task the team has been set and its timescale will often determine who should lead the team. But the requirements of the task alone are not enough; the team as a group has needs which must be met and individuals within the team have their own needs. People make statements such as 'What

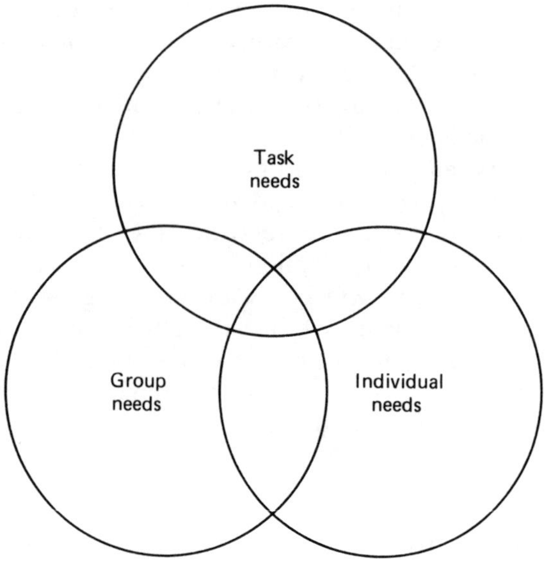

Figure 6.1 The three-circle model

we need is leadership' or 'The team needs direction' when they are articulating what the team as a whole feels is lacking. Sometimes teams feel they need support, or feedback, or better communication and they look to the leader for all these things. Within the team, individuals also have their own needs – remember Maslow's hierarchy of needs (Chapter 4). The leader needs to be aware of individual needs and fulfil these as well.

Adair (1983) expanded on the three-circle model by suggesting a number of questions the leader of a team might consider in each of the areas identified in Figure 6.1 when looking at the structure of a team. Adair himself carried out the process shown in Figure 6.2 when performing an 'organization survey' on the Dioceses of York and Chichester as a management consultant.

In summary, a leader has to be all things to all people. He or she has to balance the interrelated demands of the task and the team as well as those of individual team members. This means being directive when it is necessary; giving praise and constructive feedback when people need it; ensuring everyone and everything is operating to its full potential.

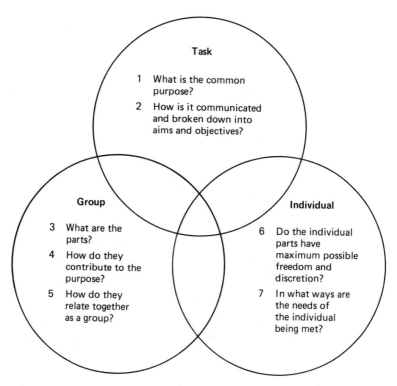

Figure 6.2 Development of the three-circle model of leadership (Adair, 1983)

INVESTIGATE

● *Think of a team of which you are a member. Does the leader consider the needs of the task, the team and the individual? In which areas is he or she (a) strongest, (b) weakest? Does the three-circle model help you to identify where this person may be lacking in leadership skills?*

Setting objectives

Just because you are clear about what the team has to achieve — its allotted task — does not necessarily mean that all the members of the team either understand this or necessarily agree with it. Very early in forming a team you need to allocate time to set objectives which everyone is clear about and which can be realistically achieved. The whole team has to be involved in this if you are to get agreement and commitment from everyone and avoid too destructive a 'storming' phase later on.

Alison was asked to head up a team to look at staff development in a small company. She was given a budget for training and three members of staff from different parts of the company to work with her. At their first meeting, she explained their objectives as being to use the budget to provide the maximum amount of essential training within the next twelve months.

At the second meeting she encountered considerable resistance to her ideas although she thought everyone had agreed with what she had said earlier. Tina, from Sales, claimed that most of the budget should be used for training her staff since, unless sales improved, company financial objectives would not be met. John argued strongly for management training to improve performance; Krish insisted that customer service staff badly needed training since they were often the first contact for potential customers. The meeting broke up without anything being agreed and with each member of the team feeling personally aggrieved.

At the next meeting Alison suggested they went back to basics and agree what their objective was in general terms before looking at ways in which they could achieve it.

Organizational objectives are often deliberately vague. At the operational, team level objectives need to be clarified and the team's resources and constraints determined. Once the team has agreed on its overall objectives, the business of putting together an action plan to achieve those objectives is the next step.

In the example above, the team's main constraint was financial, so they went on to look at training options which would not require money, such as in-service training. They identified people in the organization who could contribute to training others and act as mentors to junior staff. They drew up a training plan for each Department within the overall budget and also made recommendations for the budget to be increased in the following year. They also set up ways in which the training and its effectiveness could be monitored and measured and built in a number of review points so that changes to the original action plan could be made in the light of experience.

Monitoring and evaluating progress

Most teams are drawn together to work over a period of time — anything from a few months to years. One reason for setting objectives is that, over time, the team can check on its progress towards those objectives and, if necessary, make adjustments to the original plan.

Things change. Even in a matter of months a team may find that their original plan was too ambitious or that unexpected hitches keep occurring which slow down their progress. Key people may leave the organization and not be replaced immediately, or at all; a sudden crisis may erupt, throwing the team off course; there may be a senior management re-shuffle and priorities may change. Teams can build in 'slack' for unpredictable events and hold-ups but they do not know when or where these will occur. So it is very important for the team to take time at regular, scheduled intervals to check on how it is progressing.

However, setting aside time for review is not particularly productive unless you have some way of measuring progress, and you need to establish some kind of monitoring process early on. Ideally, all objectives should be measurable and you and your team should aim to set out not only what you intend to achieve, but how you can tell whether you have achieved it.

Let us take some objectives and see how they might be measured. For example, a team might have objectives to:

- Provide all staff with a desk-top computer within six months.
- Reduce production faults by 50 per cent.
- Decrease customer complaints to a minimum.
- Improve staff morale.

The first objective is relatively easy to measure – but how do you know you will achieve the objective within six months if you do not have some interim goals? For example, to provide 25 per cent of staff with desk-top computers by February, 40 per cent by the end of March and so on. Regular reviews can easily check on progress in this case and identify problems of meeting the final target.

The second objective, reducing faults, sounds as if it could be measured, but how much is 50 per cent? You would need at least a base monthly figure of reported faults as a yardstick so that you could check on whether faults were being reduced over the period and that the rate of reduction was being maintained and improved in line with your objective.

And how do you measure customer complaints? Are they all reported or are some anecdotal? You would need to set up a system to record the complaints and probably qualify these as 'serious', 'less serious' and so on. You would then need to monitor the rate of complaints over time to evaluate whether they were decreasing.

The final objective of improving staff morale is much more difficult to measure and should really be avoided at all costs unless you can specify how you will go about this and how you will measure progress. As you saw in Chapter 4, individuals value different rewards and are motivated by different things. There is no 'Staff Morale Improver' which you can buy off the shelf. And how do you measure the improvement? By increased production or better service, by happier people, by less absenteeism, lateness or illness . . .?

The main tasks for your team, therefore, in relation to objectives are to:

- Clarify and agree overall objectives.
- Consider options for achieving objectives.
- Set out, step by step, how the team plans to meet their objectives.
- Agree how to measure progress.
- Set a timescale and establish review points.
- Monitor and evaluate progress against measures.
- Adjust plans if necessary.

Running team meetings

The most usual way of communicating between team members is to hold regular meetings. These should also appear in your action plan and should not be held only at review points. Meetings fulfil a number of purposes (see Pinder, 1980):

- for making decisions as a team on policy or action;
- to help someone in the team or outside it make a decision;
- to provide support and help for team members or other people;
- to provide information and/or feedback on progress;
- to obtain or pool information;
- to solve a problem;
- to air grievances;
- to throw up new or creative ideas.

INVESTIGATE

- *Think about the last three meetings you attended. Which of the above purposes did they serve? (They may serve one or more purposes.)*

All team meetings should have one or more purposes and, for this reason, should have a written agenda so that everyone knows what they are going to discuss. As the chair of the meeting, you should aim to keep to the agenda so that valuable time is not wasted. (There is an exercise at the end of the chapter which can help you to cost your time and determine, in financial terms, how much of it you can afford to spend in meetings.) It is helpful to everyone not only to state the starting time of the meeting – and keep to it – but to state the finishing time, and keep to that as well.

Someone should keep notes of team meetings which may be circulated afterwards, ideally identifying individuals who agreed to take any kind of action before the next meeting and recording any decisions reached.

The control of the meeting should be with the chair, and this means allowing everyone to put their point of view but not allowing individuals to ramble or overstate their case. Conflict or grievance expressed at meetings can sometimes be dealt with more successfully outside the meeting, involving the participants only.

The place in which you hold meetings is important. Rooms which are too small, too noisy, too hot, too cold, badly ventilated or poorly and uncomfortably furnished will affect people adversely and the meeting is likely to be less successful than if these 'comfort' factors had been attended to. You may combine meetings with lunch − or, as many executives now do, with breakfast − or provide refreshments at the start of the meeting.

People complain about unproductive meetings for a variety of reasons. Some of these include the venue or the time, some relate to short notice about the meeting or not having seen the agenda beforehand; others relate to the lack of notes of earlier meetings, insufficient allowance of time or poor control by the chair. Pinder's rule for meetings is very simple:

> the effective meeting has a valid objective, it is worth holding and it has an effective chairperson.

Managing multicultural teams

If you work all, or most of the time with the same team of colleagues, you know each other's strengths and weaknesses. If you are part of a new team, brought together as part of a project, you will need time to get to know one another. A third − and increasing − possibility is working in a multicultural team with people of different nationalities, which brings its own challenges. Working in a multicultural team increases the number of different assumptions and expectations about working practices.

It is quite common in the UK for managers to work on after 'office' hours; in fact, it is often seen as a sign of dedication and commitment. Scandinavian managers, on the other hand, are used to finishing work at somewhere between 4.30 p.m. and 5 p.m. and consider people who stay on beyond that time as inefficient or incompetent.

In the USA and the UK, team members usually refer to each other by their first names. This is not the case in Germany and some Scandinavians expect to be called by their last name only. Hungarians reverse the order of their names so that their first name comes last.

Even assumptions about leadership and authority can differ quite widely amongst European member states.

> Team leaders in the Netherlands, Scandinavia and the UK adopt a more participative and consultative style of leadership than their counterparts in Germany. Dutch managers are usually fairly relaxed about who is, or who should be, in charge; Germans, however, operate within a much more formal hierarchical structure and the French do not expect their decisions to be questioned when they are in a position of authority.

A further complexity with multicultural teams is created by language. While English is considered to be the 'lingua franca' in the business world, not everyone can be expected to speak or understand it to the same extent. This convention of conducting business in English has made English-speakers lazy about acquiring skills in languages other than their own. There is a considerable danger that not everyone in a multicultural team shares the same understanding about problems and decisions or that some people, for whom English is a second language, cannot express themselves adequately. Forming a multicultural team is likely to take more time and a greater degree of sensitivity from the participants than you would expect when creating a team with shared cultural experience.

The benefits of teams

Many of us are so used to working as part of a team that we fail to recognize what benefits accrue from effective teamwork and the dynamism which well-managed teams bring to organizations. As you saw in Chapter 5, people working in groups draw upon each other's strengths to complement individual weaknesses. Team spirit, in itself, can act as a strong motivating force for personal improvement and for loyalty to the employing organization. Working in teams affords the opportunity to develop new areas of competence and different skills, and failure, as well as success, can be shared.

The concept of team roles helps to identify imbalance in groupings of employees and where there are gaps which need to be filled – this knowledge can contribute towards your Human Resource Audit and inform future recruitment, selection and development of staff. Shortfalls in communication can be highlighted both within the team itself and between one team and another, increasing awareness of areas outside its own sphere of responsibility and generating general understanding of the wider organizational context.

Summary

Effective teams are characterized by their ability to establish, and work towards, clear goals and by supportive membership, mutual trust, skilful leadership and good relations with other teams and work groups. They depend on effective recruitment, selection and training of team members, high morale and creativity, clear aims and appropriate reward systems.

Although you may not be able to select the particular team members you would wish to have, by evaluating the strengths and weaknesses of existing team members, you can develop a successful team.

Team leadership is not – and should not be – always vested in an individual by virtue of his or her place in the organizational hierarchy. It may be shared between people with appropriate expertise or abilities and should be determined by the specific needs of the task, the individuals in the team and the team itself. Team leaders are also responsible for ensuring that objectives are clarified, agreed and reviewed frequently. By regular monitoring and evaluation of progress towards agreed objectives, plans can be changed in the light of developments.

Teams need to communicate within the group, and meetings are often the most convenient way of doing this. Meetings should have a recognized purpose, such as reviewing progress, providing information, problem-solving or idea generation. They are costly in terms of time and need to be productive.

Finally, managers need to be aware of the particular problems facing multicultural teams where members do not share common experiences, working practices or even language.

Activities

1 For a team of which you are either the leader or an active member, identify its strengths and weaknesses in terms of:
(a) its effectiveness;
(b) its membership;
(c) its leadership.
What can you do about the weaknesses?

2 For a team of which you are the leader or an active member, set out its:
(a) general objective;
(b) operational plan;

(c) measures of progress;
(d) systems of monitoring and evaluation of progress.

3

Complete the following activity to see how much your time is worth:

Annual salary £

Add commission, allowances, values of any benefits such as company car, private health care etc. £

Add 25 per cent of this total for health, pension fund, National Insurance etc. £

Add 100 per cent of this total for overheads (office, heat, light, travel, secretary, administration etc.) £

Total £

Divide total by number of WORKING days per year (i.e. less holidays and weekends) £

Divide result by 8 (hours per day) £

Divide result by 60 (minutes per hour) £

References and further reading

Adair, J. (1983) *Effective Leadership*, Pan Books, London

Belbin, R. M. (1981, latest edition 1991) *Management Teams: Why They Succeed or Fail*, Butterworth-Heinemann, Oxford

Belbin, R. M. (1993) *The Management of Team Roles*, Butterworth-Heinemann, Oxford

Pinder, T. H. (1980) Effective speaking. *Occupational Therapy*, May

Woodcock, M. (1989) *Team Development Manual*, Gower, London

Woodcock, M. and Francis, D. (1990) *Organisation Development through Teambuilding*, Gower, London

7 Appraising and developing people

Introduction

Since the mid-1980s it has been widely recognized that the training and development of staff should be a major item on any organization's agenda. The Institute of Personnel Management (IPM) has drawn up a series of codes of good practice for employers which embody aims, policies and guidelines for implementation; one of these, called *Continuous Development: People and Work*, states in its introduction:

> 'continuous development' is self-directed, lifelong learning. Continuous development policies are policies first to allow and then to facilitate such learning at work, through work itself.

It goes on to state that:

> 'Successful continuous development demands:
> - rapid and effective communication of priority operational needs;
> - the availability of appropriate learning facilities and resources as a normal part of working life;
> - recognition by each employee that he or she shares ownership of any organizational collective learning plan;
> - recognition by each employee that he or she is able to create some personal development plan;
> - that all strategic and tactical operational plans fully take into account the learning implications for the employees affected;
> - clear understanding by everyone of their responsibilities.'

So what does this mean for you both as an employee of the organization and as a manager? It means that you have a responsibility for your own self-development and for the training and development of the people you manage. This involves identifying, defining and assessing the competences of individuals, including yourself; providing ways for people and yourself to learn and develop skills; and reviewing your own and your staff's development needs and career aspirations. It also involves establishing, defining and reviewing objectives and performance measures, looking at the advantages and disadvantages of existing development provision and investigating new approaches.

In order to assess the competence of your staff and set objectives for improvement, you need to set up some kind of staff appraisal system. This should be as formal as possible, even if your organization does not have its own appraisal scheme. Appraisal does not only involve assessment and objective-setting; it involves you in giving your staff constructive feedback on their performance and helping them to increase their potential. It is a contract between you and the individual.

The first part of this chapter, therefore, will look at self-development before going on to discuss appraisal systems and the training and development of your staff. In this chapter we will be looking at:

- Planning your own self-development.
- Appraisal systems.
- Giving feedback.
- Training and developing your staff.

Management in practice

Self-development

What have you done recently to increase your competence as a manager? Like many others, you might reply:

'I was sent on the company's three-day leadership course last May.'

or

'We have an in-service training course on selection interviewing – I went on that.'

or

'I'm thinking about going on a course on managing time.'

Most managers who work in organizations without a stated management development policy manage to get some training in rather a piecemeal way; perhaps they hear of a course, or there is a note about one in the company newsletter or on the noticeboard. 'That looks interesting ...' they think, and put their names down for it. Some managers are more proactive and seek out training opportunities before trying to persuade their employers to pay for them; others are forced to fund their own training.

The recent government initiative 'Investors in People' (IIP) was launched in October 1991 in an attempt to persuade employers to take an interest in training and developing their employees. In order to qualify as Investors in People, organizations have to make a public commitment from the top to develop all employees to achieve their business objectives; they have regularly to review the training and development needs of all employees and take action to train and develop staff on recruitment and throughout their employment; they also have to evaluate their investment in training and development to assess achievement and improve future effectiveness.

For some organizations, the good practice encouraged by IIP was already part of their policy; companies such as Distillers and Vintners of Essex and Nissan Motor Manufacturing (UK) claimed that they needed to make only a few alterations to current practice in order to comply with IIP standards. Many others have failed to meet the very high standards demanded by the initiative.

So, if you are a manager in an organization that is not recognized as an Investor in People and has no stated staff development policy, what should you do? If you have an appraisal system, this can be the opportunity for you to raise with your appraiser where you think your weaknesses lie and in what areas you need training and development. And this should include development not only in the job you are currently doing, but for your next step up on the career ladder.

What is your next step up? Many managers have no clear idea of career progression either within the organization for which they currently work or beyond that organization. Today's unsettled work environment may mean the need to re-train and change direction, not always upwards, several times during working life.

The BBC has introduced an imaginative programme to help their staff manage their careers. They run career planning workshops each year as part of a wider career development programme, recognizing the need for individuals to take responsibility for their own careers now that joining the organization no longer means a job for life. The Career Point programme not only runs workshops but offers staff the chance to identify their own skills, interests and

> work values through an interactive computer program. There are also opportunities for career counselling or specialist counselling, including psychometric testing. Moreover, they operate a Job Shop for staff who are about to be made redundant which helps them to match their skills to jobs outside the BBC. (Arkin, 1991)

Planning your own career and self-development involves acquiring information about jobs inside your own organization and possibilities outside it. It involves systematically assessing your own strengths and weaknesses, and, where possible, getting someone else at work who knows you well to evaluate these for you. It means matching your strengths to the requirements of other jobs and reducing your weaknesses through training and skill acquisition. It requires a lot of self-investigation, complete honesty and determination.

INVESTIGATE

● *Try to get hold of the job description for a post which you aspire to in your organization. With complete honesty, evaluate your personal strengths and weaknesses against the requirements of the job. What do you need to do next?*

You need to identify your own goals in career terms, set yourself some clear and realistic objectives and plan how you are going to achieve these within a given timescale. As with any plan, such as those we described in the previous chapter, you also need to review it regularly and make adjustments in light of a changing situation.

It is particularly important to make your objectives realistically achievable. Failure to reach them will only set you back more than you expect. However, there are plenty of opportunities for developing yourself if you have commitment to your plan; some of these will be suggested in the section on training and developing your staff.

> Sir Leonard Peach, former personnel chief at IBM, suggests that employees should play a larger part in their own appraisal. Amongst his recommendations is that all employees keep a log book which acts as their personnel record. This, he argues, both empowers employees and releases busy managers from some of their responsibilities for appraisal.

Appraisal systems

The benefits of appraisal

Although appraisal could be seen to come after training and development in that it is designed to measure performance against objectives, a system has to be in place to agree the objectives in the first place.

There are a number of reasons why appraisal is necessary from the viewpoints of the organization, the manager and the employee.

The **organization** benefits from:

- standard information about its employees;
- the facility to develop individuals based on appraisal information;
- being able to plan its human resource needs more accurately.

The **manager** benefits from:

- objective guidelines for assessing staff;
- gaining a better understanding of staff needs;
- improved relationships with staff.

The **individual** benefits from:

- an opportunity to discuss his or her work objectively;
- the ability to evaluate performance;
- consideration of future training and development needs;
- improved relationships with his or her manager.

Any organization needs to know the strengths and weaknesses of its employees; any manager needs this information about the people who work in his or her department; and any individual needs to know how he or she is performing. A good appraisal scheme can satisfy all these needs.

You may already operate an appraisal scheme in your organization. If so, this section should help you to assess its current benefits and, if necessary, identify areas for improvement. If, however, you are setting up an appraisal system for the first time, this section will give you some guidelines but you may need to seek professional help from somewhere like the Institute of Personnel Management or get hold of the booklet on 'Employee Appraisal' (No. 11) from the Advisory, Conciliation and Arbitration Service (ACAS).

An appraisal system helps you as a manager to learn more about your employees, their problems and needs and how their aspirations are being fulfilled by their job. It can help you to increase their motivation by discovering the satisfying and less satisfying aspects of their jobs in the opinion of the individuals who perform them. It can help to improve individual performance and productivity and, thus, increase your job satisfaction as the person accountable for your area of responsibility.

An appraisal system in operation

An appraisal system should have the following objectives (adapted from Hunt, 1986):

- to provide a two-way boss–subordinate review of the subordinate's performance over a period of time (usually one year);
- to feed back to senior management information on the performance of employees or of a group of employees, such as a Project Team;
- to tell individuals what their strengths and weaknesses are;
- to provide relevant information for reviewing salary, promotion and other rewards;
- to help with identifying training and development needs for individuals;
- to provide an inventory of skills, competence, qualifications, talents etc;
- to provide input for human resource planning, succession planning, career planning and other similar devices.

INVESTIGATE

- *If you currently operate an appraisal system in your organization, does it fulfil these objectives?*
- *If you do not have a formal appraisal system, how do you and your organization meet any of the objectives above? Is this satisfactory?*

In a formal appraisal system, there needs to be an assessment of the individual's performance over a period of time. Self-assessment by the individual is one way of measuring this, as is peer assessment or your own evaluation of how a person is performing in their current job. However, objective measures of performance are preferable and much fairer to the individual. Has he or she achieved an overall, agreed standard of performance against criteria which were known in advance? The job description is an obvious point of reference here, providing it is up to date and, if possible, includes performance measures, or, if the team has set itself objectives which can be measured, the individual can be assessed against these. Unless the individual is actually aware of the standards against which he or she is being measured, the appraisal is unfair and invalid.

Having agreed the objectives and measured the individual against these, that person's strengths and weaknesses in relation to the criteria can be identified. Ideally, these should be set down in writing or on a special appraisal form in agreement with the person being appraised. Thereafter, the appraiser and the person being appraised should discuss and agree (a) what specific training and development the individual needs to remedy weak areas and (b) what his or her objectives should be over the period before the next appraisal or interim review. An interim review is often necessary since most formal appraisals are carried out on an annual basis. Such reviews serve to monitor progress towards the next set of objectives.

The manager needs to establish a relationship of trust with the individual and all appraisal discussions and records should be confidential between those two. In some organizations it is customary for a summary of the appraisal, agreed with the individual, to contribute towards promotion, re-grading or salary review processes: in others, the full appraisal record is used. It is essential, in these cases, that the individual has seen the appraisal summary or report before it goes further.

This contribution to the advancement − or otherwise − of the individual through appraisal has been criticized. The atmosphere of trust between appraiser and appraisee is threatened if not destroyed by the knowledge that a poor appraisal may cost the latter promotion or a salary increase. Some managers hesitate to tell the truth about their subordinates' performance because they dislike upsetting the subordinate or because poor performance may reflect on their own managerial adequacy. In other cases, subordinates may feel considerable dissatisfaction if they do not receive expected rewards and blame their appraiser − rightly or wrongly − for his or her appraisal report.

Giving feedback

Although part of the appraisal system will be involved in getting the individual to make a self-appraisal of his or her performance, everyone needs feedback on their performance from others if there is to be any improvement.

We all engage in appraisal on an everyday basis, particularly with people we know well and within our own close domestic circle. We make judgements about whether people are performing above or below our expectations. We comment to others on the performance of the public transport system, the state of the roads, the content of television programmes, the performance of our bosses and subordinates, the way our children behave, the actions of government and the law and so on. Yet, in Western cultures, we hesitate to tell most people about their weaknesses to their faces. And, for many people, it is difficult for them to praise people directly as well.

Giving feedback in an appraisal situation requires sensitivity and openness on the part of the manager. You may have to tell someone that they are not performing well enough and no one likes criticism, even when it is deserved. As the appraiser, you have to be sure that it is not your fault, or the organization's that the person is not performing as well as expected. Not infrequently, the appraisal reveals that lack of essential training or lack of resources and time are contributing significantly to below-average performance.

Gil knew he had a difficult time ahead when it came to appraising Andy. The man just wasn't up to the job and his team were performing less well than any of the others – they never seemed to produce results. He had had to make a presentation to the Board earlier in the year and, by all accounts, it had been disastrous.

Andy was defensive, 'It's all this extra work I'm expected to do,' he complained, 'it doesn't leave me enough time. And everyone else in my team has been here longer than me and knows what they're doing.' Through careful questioning, Gil discovered that the Sales Manager had asked Andy to prepare a detailed sales plan for the department which Gil knew nothing about. He also realized that Andy had not been given any induction when he joined the company and that, when he had asked to be sent on a course to improve his presentation skills, Gil's assistant had turned this down. Much of Andy's poor performance was not his own fault.

Carly was dreading her annual appraisal. She knew that the parents of two of the children in her class had objected formally about how much homework she was giving out and that, despite all her efforts, the end-of-term show had been poorly organized. Her Junior Choir had excelled themselves at the Festival but, on the other hand, classwork was a bit behind and she was always late with her reports.

She was pleasantly surprised when Miss Bowles praised her not only about the choir's success but also about her work with two children with learning difficulties, and felt relaxed enough to admit her own shortcomings in other parts of her job. She agreed that she had taken on too much and set her targets too high initially and that she needed to prioritize her work and manage her time better. Together they agreed on her objectives for the following year, with interim objectives which Miss Bowles would review with her at the end of each term. Carly also agreed to attend a time management course which was being run locally – she wished she'd known about this before. She left her appraisal

> with a sense of relief that they had been able to discuss her weak areas objectively and identify ways of improvement in these and she was buoyed up by the recognition of what she had done well.

'The praise sandwich' has long been a cornerstone of giving feedback – praising the subordinate at the outset for good performance, followed by a constructive discussion of areas of weakness and concluding with a restatement of his or her strengths. An appraisal which concentrates almost solely on areas of poor performance will result in the person being appraised feeling resentful and poorly motivated to improve.

INVESTIGATE

● *When did you last praise someone for their performance at work?*

Identifying competence in performance

Although objectives, measures and standards can be used as benchmarks against which to measure an individual's competence, there is another factor which was identified in the recent research undertaken by the Management Charter Initiative (1992), which they called 'personal competence'. This factor can be broken down into the following attributes.

1 Planning to optimize the achievement of results by:
   (a) showing concern for excellence;
   (b) setting and prioritizing objectives;
   (c) monitoring and responding to actual against planned activities.
2 Managing others to optimize results through:
   (a) showing sensitivity to others;
   (b) relating to others;
   (c) obtaining the commitment of others;
   (d) presenting oneself positively to others.
3 Managing oneself to optimize results through:
   (a) showing self-confidence and personal drive;
   (b) managing personal emotions and stress;
   (c) managing personal learning and development.
4 Using intellect to optimize results through:
   (a) collecting and analysing information;
   (b) identifying and applying concepts;
   (c) taking decisions.

These personal competences may be regarded as higher-level competences than those required for adequate performance of the job. While they relate to managerial competence, they are equally applicable to any employee and can be used to identify people who have above-average competence or are likely to be suitable for promotion or other advancement.

INVESTIGATE

• *Go through the list above and make a self-assessment of your personal competence as a manager. Did you identify any areas which need strengthening? What are you going to do about these?*

Training and developing your staff

> British companies, particularly medium-sized companies, starting from 1993 plan to spend more on training supervisors than on training senior managers.

For many managers, embarking on a programme of staff development for the people in their area of responsibility alerts them to their own needs for training and development. As a manager, you are accountable for the performance of your staff; your success depends on their ability. Better trained staff should increase efficiency and even productivity by reducing fatigue and wastage.

The starting point is to identify training and development needs for individual members of staff. Again, as with recruitment and team-building, this involves analysing the individual's competences in relation to the present job and skills not currently used. There are commercial Training Needs Analyses available for this purpose, but, if you know your staff well, you should be able to make a very good estimate of what is needed yourself.

Each individual for whom you are responsible is likely to fall into one of three categories in relation to their competence to perform the job. These are:

- Competent to perform current job.
- Not yet competent to perform current job.
- Better than competent at performing current job.

For each category you can provide development as shown in Figure 7.1.

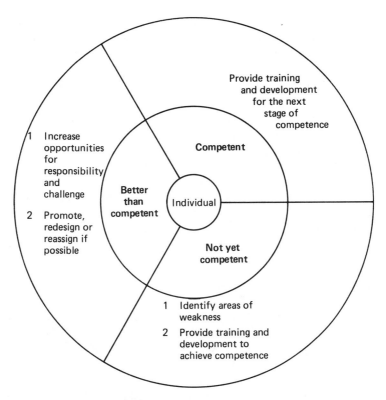

Figure 7.1 Training needs of individuals

You have to enable your staff to 'grow' in the organization. Somebody who is better than competent in their present job will soon become frustrated and will leave, reduce their performance or become a source of conflict through their personal dissatisfaction. You need to provide recognition of their value and help them to achieve higher objectives. It is not always possible to promote people but you can increase their job satisfaction through delegation or redesigning their jobs (see Chapters 4 and 9).

For those who are not yet competent – and note that we did not use the word 'incompetent' since this implies that they are unlikely to improve – you have to provide opportunities for the individual to develop in the areas of weakness. Most managers find this relatively easy and satisfying unless there is truly no hope of improvement.

The third category – those who are performing their jobs competently – are too often ignored. Even employees can be reluctant to go beyond what is acceptable – doing 'a fair day's work for a fair day's pay'. Unless they can see rewards for achievement which they value, there is no incentive to improve performance. Managers, too, can be reluctant to expend time and energy on people who are performing up to standard. Moving beyond current competence involves both the employee and the manager agreeing on a development plan which the former sees as being in his or her best interests.

Training and development opportunities at the place of work

Induction Induction might seem to follow naturally from recruitment and selection, which it should, but it is also the initial training and development any employee deserves on joining the organization. It should not be just about the demands of the specific job; it should introduce the newcomer to the way in which the organization and this particular department is structured, what makes this organization different from others, what the organization has achieved and the kind of behaviour which is accepted by the organization. Induction is the first step in encouraging commitment to what the organization does.

> Safeway, the supermarket chain, introduced a competence-based induction programme, known as 'Head Start', to train between 12,000 and 15,000 new staff during 1992. The programme includes three days' training 'off-the-job' and covers areas of knowledge such as hygiene legislation as well as more specific, job-related tasks. Once the induction is completed, staff are assessed over a 12-week period on their competence in the job; those deemed to be competent are given a pay rise.

There is also a need at induction to explain how the department 'works', what goes on in it, who the people are who work in it, what the reward system is and so on.

> As part of its effort to improve customer service, Wessex Water Authority introduced a six-week induction programme for all its customer service staff. The programme included field training, with staff working with plumbers and sewer repair teams to find out what the jobs entailed. There were sessions on the company's water, sewerage and billing systems as well as training on dealing with customers. The staff welcomed the programme and felt more confident about dealing with a much wider range of enquiries than they had before.

Induction is rarely given to temporary or short-term staff in the misguided belief that they will not care much about the organization as a whole and that they are just there to do the job. However, many organizations rely heavily on temporary staff and use them on a regular basis. They need training if they are going to be effective.

Where companies have a high proportion of temporary staff, it pays off to offer induction training prior to starting work. TNT Express Worldwide has a policy of encouraging long-term relationships with temporary clerical support staff so that they will come back when the company needs them. Where possible, TNT provides practical 'hands-on' experience of the job for which temporary help is needed and new staff are introduced to the place and the people where they will be working. They are given a copy of the company's manual, 'Welcome to TNT' and a copy of the company's quality strategy.

INVESTIGATE

- *What induction training do you and your organization provide for new staff? Is it adequate? How might it be improved?*

The following are some simple and inexpensive ways in which you can provide training and development for your staff within the organization.

Mentoring Mentoring is a form of training and development which has been popular in Japan for some time. A mentor is someone, usually a work colleague at the same or a higher level than the individual, for whom he or she is responsible, to whom the individual can go to discuss work-related issues. There is a sense in which the mentoring relationship is similar to that of the 'master–pupil' relationship in medieval times; the pupil is learning from the mentor's experience and the mentor's role is to encourage and nurture his or her protégé. Mentors can pass on practical insight derived from experience and can pick up on new ideas and attitudes. They can help their protégés to set themselves realistic expectations and steer them in the right direction as far as their career aspirations are concerned. It can, and should, be a mutually rewarding experience. Many people value being able to pass on what they know, particularly when this is appreciated and others benefit from their knowledge and experience.

An individual may have more than one informal mentor, different people to whom he or she can go for advice and help. This tends to be a proactive approach on the part of the individual who deliberately seeks out others from whom to learn. It may be a formal mentoring arrangement whereby mentors are assigned to new staff as they are recruited. Both forms of mentoring have their benefits and disadvantages. A mentor chosen by his or her protégé will have the advantage over one who is 'imposed'. On the other hand, not everyone is proactive in seeking a mentor and a formalized system at least ensures everyone has someone to whom they can go.

It is unfortunate that, although many organizations encourage informal and formal mentoring, few provide training for mentors, make time available in which to undertake this responsibility or give rewards. An untrained mentor can have disastrous effects on new staff and can actually reinforce bad practice rather than encouraging good performance. Mentoring meetings need to be arranged beforehand, programmed into the diary and have a clear agenda relating to the protégé's needs. Rewards for mentoring are often intrinsic, in that mentors value the increased responsibility, whereas in Japan some companies reward the mentor when the protégé achieves promotion.

Job or work rotation This involves staff trying out a number of different jobs or different parts of the same job to get an understanding of other kinds of task and of how they all fit together. In either case, someone will have to be responsible for training the person in the new job or work.

Secondment This is a more formal type of job rotation in which a member of staff is seconded to another job on a short- or long-term basis, perhaps while someone is ill or when a member of staff has left.

Special assignments or projects These can involve the person in different work which may suit that person's particular skills.

'Sitting by Nellie' This form of training, which is similar to mentoring, exists in many organizations, notably those involved with production or manufacturing. The trainee is assigned to an experienced member of staff who *should* be given training in how to train and time in which to do it (but often is not).

Coaching To be effective, this form of training needs to be planned and time should be allowed for the coach to develop staff. It involves consciously seeking out opportunities for developing people, training the person to do the job and giving him or her impartial feedback on performance. It has the advantage of developing the coach as well as the trainee.

There are many other forms of training and staff development – demonstrations, discussion groups, presentations, simulations, assessment centres, computer-aided training, action learning groups, in-tray exercises – but they all need to be seen in an overall training and development context. Part of your job as a manager is not only to identify training needs but to plan and implement a cost-effective and ongoing training programme, using resources both inside the organization and outside it as well.

Staff development outside the organization

Many organizations use a combination of in-house specialized training and external training providers: the balance is up to you, the organization, its needs, the needs of the individual and the training budget.

The range of external providers is immense, including local colleges and universities, business schools, commercial training organizations, professional institutions and employers' federations. Your first contact when looking for external training provision should be your local Training and Enterprise Council (TEC), or Local Enterprise Council (LEC) if you are based in Scotland.

Some organizations, such as those involved in the hotel and catering industry, clothing, construction and road transport have their own Industry Training Boards (ITBs) which encourage industry-related training by line managers. There are also a number of voluntary training arrangements, such as the Local Government Training Board and the Dairy Trade Federation but, for general training purposes, the government has established local Training and Enterprise Councils. TECs/LECs will encourage employers to become Investors in People and they act as 'brokers' between organizations that have identified training needs and training providers on a local and national basis.

One of the most important training developments in the 1990s has been the emergence of National Vocational Qualifications (NVQs or SVQs in Scotland), actively promoted and supported by the government. These have been developed in response to the confusing array of qualifications supposedly related to organizational needs. Vocational qualifications are *directly* related to the needs of the employer.

The retail chain W. H. Smith offers an NVQ award for its 13,000 shop assistants which it runs in addition to its own training programme.

The Youth Hostel Association has played a part in developing NVQs for the accommodation, leisure and recreation industry.

Competence-based materials, compatible with the NVQ system, have been produced for use on the Association of Accounting Technician's examination syllabus.

The National Retail Training Council and City and Guilds have developed NVQ Certificates for supervisors and managers in the retail trade. The competence-based qualification has no pre-entry requirements, age or time restrictions, takes into account previous experience and allows candidates to work at their own pace.

A competence-based NVQ Certificate is now available by distance-learning for managers in the National Health Service.

INVESTIGATE

- *Find out what training opportunities exist locally which might be of use to you in developing yourself and your staff.*

Not all external training needs to involve people being away from work: indeed, with the advent of NVQs, it is preferable that individuals remain at work while they are undergoing training. One effect of the introduction of NVQs/SVQs has been the development of managers as assessors for these qualifications. Instead of sending staff off to the local college or buying in training from outside, organizations can train their own staff and assess them in the workplace. There are also a wide range of distance and open learning training packages available, many of which only involve people in off-site training outside normal working hours.

Help available

Apart from TECs/LECs and Industrial Training Boards or industry-specific training organizations, the following organizations can provide information and support on training matters:

- The Institute of Personnel Management
- The Industrial Society

- The British Association for Commercial and Industrial Education
- The Institute of Manpower Studies

Local libraries are also a useful source of information on provision of training and development near your place of work.

Summary

Continuous self- and staff-development are essential to continuous performance improvement. Present government initiatives have recognized this fact and provided encouragement for training and development, unfortunately not supported by financial incentives for organizations.

Your own self-development needs to be related to your personal strengths and weaknesses and to your individual career aspirations. This requires planning your career progression, either within your present organization or outside it, and setting your career goals.

Appraisal systems should be designed to focus employees on both their short- and long-term objectives and career goals. Well-designed appraisal systems benefit the organization, managers and individuals in different ways and need to fulfill certain key objectives if they are to be successful. Appraisal is concerned with setting objectives for individuals for an agreed period and monitoring progress towards these objectives on a regular basis in an atmosphere of trust and cooperation between the appraiser and the individual.

This trust and cooperation also involves being able to provide staff with constructive feedback on their performance, whether it be good or bad. This feedback will only be effective if performance itself can be measured in ways which are truly objective and which can identify above-and below-average competence in individuals.

Programmes of training and development for staff need to be related to individual training needs and aspirations. Induction training and mentoring are two methods of providing training for new staff, although mentoring arrangements often continue beyond the initial training period.

There is a wide range of training and development opportunities which can be provided by the organization or by other providers. This external training can be industry- or sector-specific, or it may be more general in focus. There are also opportunities for managers to devise competence-based programmes leading to the award of an NVQ/SVQ and for them to be trained as assessors in this form of staff development.

Activities

1 Draw up a personal action plan for your own career development over the next five years. Be realistic about your objectives and ensure that they reflect short-term achievements as well as long-term goals.

2 Either suggest improvements to an existing appraisal system in your own organization, or design an appraisal system which would meet the objectives outlined in this chapter.

3 Identify the training needs for individuals within your area of responsibility. What provision for training could you provide from within the organization?

4 Draw up a list of training provisions which would meet the needs of staff you identified in (3) above, using internal and external training resources where appropriate.

5 Draw up an induction programme for new staff.

References

Arkin, A. (1991) The BBC's Career Planning Programme. *PM Plus*, December, pp. 16–17

Hunt, J. W. (1986) *Managing People at Work*, 2nd edn, McGraw-Hill, Maidenhead

Institute of Personnel Management *Continuous Development: People and Work*. (regularly published) Institute of Personnel Management Code of Practice, IPM, London

Management Charter Initiative (1992) *Management Standards*, Management Charter Initiative, London

Further reading

Boydell, T. (1985) *Managing Yourself*, Fontana, London

Clutterbuck, D. (1991) *Everybody Needs a Mentor*, Institute of Personnel Management, London

Ferrucci, P. (1985) *What We May Be*, Turnstone Press

Fletcher, S. (1992) *Competence-based Assessment Techniques*, Kogan Page, London

Harrison, R. (1992) *Employee Development*, Institute of Personnel Management, London

Herriot, P. (1992) *The Career Management Challenge*, Sage, London

O'Neill, B. (1991) *The Manager as an Assessor*, Industrial Society Press, London

Pedlar, M., Burgoyne, J. and Boydell, T. (1986) *A Manager's Guide to Self-Development*, McGraw-Hill, Maidenhead

Plett, P. and Lester, B. (1991) *Training for Older People: a Handbook*, International Labour Office, Geneva

Reid, M. and Barrington, H. (1992) *Training Interventions*, Institute of Personnel Management, London

Swan, W. S. (1991) *How to Do a Superior Performance Appraisal*, John Wiley, Chichester

8 Managing adversity

Introduction

Although managing people is an exhilarating experience, particularly when everything is going well, there are some parts of the job which most managers would prefer to avoid. These are the times when people are distressed, or upset about some aspect of their job, or when there is a need to take disciplinary action over somebody's behaviour, or when it becomes necessary to make staff redundant. In many cases, it is the manager's responsibility to deal with cases of grievance or to become involved in disciplinary action when this becomes inevitable; it is also his or her responsibility to offer help and advice to staff who have work-related problems and, where necessary, to recommend that they seek professional advice. Particularly in a time of severe recession, there is also the increasing possibility that staff may have to be made redundant and they will need help to retain their self-confidence and survive the experience.

This chapter deals with adversity; the kinds of problems which face all managers at some time no matter how adept and experienced they are at managing people. Obviously, if you are having to cope with disgruntled or demoralized staff most of the time, you need to think about why this is happening; the problems may be inherent in the organization or in its environment or it may be something to do with your own management style.

Managing grievance or redundancy and taking disciplinary action are all beset with legal procedures and obligations as well as with regulations specific to your own organization. Many larger organizations employ specialist staff to deal with personnel-related matters and it is their responsibility to keep up to date with the many and frequent changes in the law, particularly now that EC Directives are compounding the situation. But, even in organizations with this facility, the line manager will be involved in any formal grievance or disciplinary matters. On a day-to-day basis, you may have to deal with the first signs of trouble and, if there is no handy Personnel Department, with subsequent action.

This chapter is not designed to give you a detailed knowledge of the law governing grievance, discipline and redundancy but it aims to make you aware of the need to find out how it applies in particular situations and what kinds of formal action may be necessary. It also aims to help you deal with the early stages of adversity in the hope that more serious and prolonged problems can be avoided. The chapter will cover:

- Handling grievances.
- Sex and race discrimination.
- Harassment.
- Grievance interviews.
- Grievance procedures.
- The role of ACAS.
- Taking disciplinary action.
- Dismissal.
- Managing redundancy.
- The legal and regulatory framework.

Management in practice

Handling grievances

> A member of your staff comes to you to complain that his weekly pay packet contains less than he thinks it ought to. You remind him that he took half a day's leave earlier in the week and he goes back to work satisfied with your answer.
>
> A group of staff come to you with the complaint that your suppliers are failing to meet deadlines and work is being held up as a result. You promise to investigate the problem and reassure them that it will not affect their pay until the matter is settled. You discover their grievance is genuine and put pressure on the suppliers to conform to deadlines. Work returns to normal. (Examples from Thomson and Murray, 1976)

> Denise alleged that the store manager had made sexual gestures to her when they were alone. Another female employee made similar complaints. They complained to more senior management but no investigation occurred until, on union advice, written complaints were sent to their regional manager. Eventually all were interviewed.
>
> The manager remained at work during this time. He was told to apologize and Denise was offered a transfer. This was sex discrimination since there was a case of clear harassment, there had been a very slow response during which time the victim was left at work, and she, not the harasser, was expected to move. The employer was liable as the manager was exercising his supervisory duties when he harassed Denise. An industrial tribunal awarded compensation of £3,500 to Denise for injured feelings.

> The power of the unions and the threat of widespread strikes in industry have both decreased in the past twenty years. However, the Advisory, Conciliation and Arbitration Service (ACAS) handled 60,605 individual conciliation cases over infringement of employee rights in 1991.

A grievance begins as an expression of dissatisfaction by an individual or group of employees in respect of 'any measure or situation which directly affects or may affect the conditions of employment of one or several workers in the undertaking when that measure or situation appears contrary to the provisions of an applicable collective agreement or of an individual contract of employment, to work rules, to laws or regulations or to the custom or usage of the occupation or country' (International Labour Organisation, 1965).

A grievance usually starts with some kind of trigger in the form of management or peer action which gives rise to individual or group dissatisfaction. If the dissatisfaction is initially experienced by an individual, the person may seek allies to support him or her in their opinions or may go to his or her manager and voice the dissatisfaction. At this stage, it may be no more than a 'dissatisfaction' with some aspect of the individual's working environment which can be handled sensitively and the dissatisfaction reduced or eliminated if it is within the manager's control. If the dissatisfaction is more widespread, the kind of group cohesion described in Chapter 5 can occur and the discontent can grow accordingly. Again, it may be possible for the manager to avert this growing dissatisfaction or it may be necessary to consult with colleagues or people higher up in the organization or turn the matter over to a superior. It all depends on the extent and the level of dissatisfaction and the way in which it is handled as to whether it becomes a more formalized and serious grievance.

> At least twenty staff of a manufacturing company in Leicester claim they have been unfairly selected for redundancy and the company is facing its second series of industrial tribunals in four years. Staff also claim that redundancy payments contradicted custom and practice in the firm. An expert in this area stated that most cases that went to industrial tribunals were the result of a failure by the company to consult staff adequately about redundancy procedures.

When one of your staff comes to you with a complaint, however trivial, you need to establish all the facts as that person reports them and check these out with other people concerned. If you try to handle problems on the basis of inadequate or incorrect information, it is quite possible for you to contribute unwittingly to making them more serious. In most cases, unless you feel you are absolutely sure of all the facts surrounding a grievance, you should avoid making any comment immediately apart from promising to investigate the complaint fully — and following this up with prompt action. Ignoring a grievance can also cause it to grow. Your aim as a manager is to investigate the underlying cause of the grievance rather than to solve the immediate problem as the individual perceives it.

There are a number of factors which contribute to the extent to which a grievance may be genuine, imagined, relatively unimportant or potentially serious. These include individual and group attitudes, beliefs and perceptions about working practices and norms and the rights of employees in the organization. There are also factors concerned with the overall relationships between the parties involved — the balance of power between them and the degree of trust and openness — and the extent to which the organization and its employees are rule-bound and operate in a more or less strictly controlled working environment. The culture of the organization also has a part to play; in role-based cultures where there is well-defined and understood differentiation between what people are expected to do or not do, grievances usually relate to rules or norms being ignored or broken. In other cultures, where organizational rules are minimal and where autonomy is prevalent, grievances tend to be based on individual perceptions and interpersonal or intergroup conflict.

One way of understanding grievance is to look at the sense of deprivation or unfairness in treatment that may be felt by individuals. Dissatisfaction can be seen as the difference between what one feels one deserves and what one actually receives in the form of rewards or feedback. If past or current emotional or material rewards decrease or if expectations and realistic aspirations increase, dissatisfaction grows (Smith, 1967).

According to Bouwen and Salipante (1990) there are four distinct stages through which a grievance can pass, although the time taken at each stage will vary in individual cases. The first of these is the individual's perception of dissatisfaction or *private formulation* of a grievance. The person feels unfairly treated or perceives an action taken by someone else as being unfair. At this stage, the individual keeps his or her dissatisfaction private. When he or she decides to talk to other people about it — *public formulation* — there is a transformation of the grievance and it is likely to become distorted. At this stage, the person is looking for help and support, so they put their grievance into terms that are likely to elicit this kind of response. Instead of saying 'I don't get any recognition for all this extra work I'm doing', the person may state the grievance as 'None of us gets any recognition for all this extra work' in order to get the sympathy and support of colleagues and to make their own case stronger.

After public formulation of the grievance comes the stage of *action* which may involve a formal or informal statement of grievance to people with authority over the situation or such actions as working to rule, decreasing productivity or the level of service, calling in trade union support and so on. Finally there will be an *outcome*; the grievance may be settled or it may result in some form of loss to the individual or the organization through the ruling of an industrial tribunal.

> Of the individual complaints handled by the Arbitration, Conciliation and Advisory Service (ACAS) in 1991, 93 per cent arose from formal complaints to industrial tribunals.

Most managers will become involved at the second stage and this is why it is important to understand that what a person is telling you is likely to be formulated in such a way as to elicit a particular kind of response from you, usually in the form of support or in taking action to reduce the cause of the grievance.

So when someone comes to you with a complaint which may, or may not, be a genuine grievance, what should you do? First, you should take some kind of action and investigate the cause of the complaint — gather as much information as possible from the person who has expressed the dissatisfaction and others involved. It may be useful, depending on the severity and type of grievance and your organization's culture, to call a meeting of those involved and check on all the facts as individuals perceive them. This should clear up any misunderstandings and clarify the facts as well as create shared understanding. Sometimes, this may be all that has to be done, particularly if the grievance is interpersonal, or further action may be necessary to remove or minimize the cause.

One method of reducing the potential severity of grievance, which is becoming increasingly popular and appears to be very effective is the creation of 'peer review committees' from among employees of the organization. The person with the grievance and his or her supervisor can select a small panel from among a pool of the employee's peers who will be responsible for listening to the grievance and suggesting ways in which it might be resolved. There is a perceived fairness in this system since most people are more prepared to accept the judgement of a selection of their peers than that of a superior or even of an external agency. It can also speed up the process whereby the grievance is given a fair hearing and this can often reduce frustration created by the feeling that no one is taking any notice.

Sex and race discrimination

> A major national organization is now pressing ahead with equal opportunities training for its managers and reviewing its recruitment and selection procedures following a damages award by an industrial tribunal of £8,000 plus costs and reinstatement to one of its senior women executives.

Cases of sex discrimination considered by ACAS rose by 119 per cent and cases of race discrimination by 24 per cent in 1991. This may not reflect a growing trend in discrimination but, more likely, that employees have an increased awareness of their rights under the Sex Discrimination Acts of 1975 and 1986 and the Race Relations Act (1976). Apart from the requirement not to discriminate against individuals on the grounds of gender or race in selection, the law also states that people should be given equal opportunities and rewards once they are in employment. This includes equal pay for equal work as well as equal terms and conditions of employment for both men and women, equal promotion, training and transfer opportunities, equal benefits and equality in selection for redundancy or short-term working. Failure to avoid discrimination in any of these areas can lead to dissatisfaction, formally expressed through grievance procedures and leading to costly results for the organization.

> The Belfast planemaker, Shorts, has been involved in a seven-year equal pay battle which ended in victory for women clerical workers. An industrial tribunal stated, following a settlement with the company, that three of the original twelve claimants are entitled to the same level of pay as storemen; each received a lump sum with pay increases of up to £40 per week while other claimants received a lump sum. Shorts, which employs 9,000 people, now have to review pay relationships between various groups of employees, including undertaking a major job evaluation exercise.

It is also unlawful to discriminate on racial grounds in terms of employment and in the provision of benefits, facilities and services for employees. Employers and managers should never ignore or treat lightly grievances from members of particular racial groups on the assumption that they are over-sensitive about discrimination.

Harassment

> The European Commission has made proposals on the treatment of sexual harassment at work, accompanied by a code of practice to help employers and employees develop effective policies to combat sexual harassment.

According to a survey by the Industrial Relations Services in 1992, sexual harassment is likely to occur in most workplaces, across all sectors of employment, in large and small organizations. In nearly half the cases reported, harassers are dismissed. Under the provision of the Sex Discrimination Act 1975, as seen in the case of Denise earlier in this chapter, a woman can make a claim to an industrial tribunal if she experiences sexual harassment at work. Some organizations are taking initiatives to help women and people from ethnic minority groups to report instances of harassment at work.

> As part of its new policy on harassment at work, the BBC has introduced a sexual harassment helpline and counselling service. Staff who feel they are being harassed are encouraged to speak out and seek help from specially trained advisers.

> Elida Gibbs, a subsidiary of Unilever, has introduced a special complaints procedure intended to address the issues of sexual and racial harassment at work.

> Brighton Borough Council was cited in 1992 by the Employment Department as an example of good practice. The council defines sexual harassment as 'conduct of a sexual nature which is unwanted by the recipient which the perpetrator knows or should know is offensive'. This includes unwanted physical contact, persistent attention such as leering and jokes or verbal abuse of a sexual nature. The council has produced guidelines for managers and leaflets for all staff informing them of the policy.
>
> Every department has a network of female staff who have been trained to provide support to those who have experienced harassment. A special procedure is laid down for investigating cases, including provision for them to be resolved informally. Managers are trained to deal with issues of harassment and go on to act as trainers for other employees. (*Personnel Management*, April 1992)

Cases of reported harassment have to be taken seriously — and they do not all relate to female staff being harassed by male colleagues; the reverse can also occur. If anyone is distressed by the actions or statements of others which relate to their sex or race, or to any other personal attribute which appears to differentiate them from 'the majority', you need to act promptly and sensitively. By the time someone comes to you officially with such a complaint, that person may have suffered enough mental anguish for it to have affected their work or their health and any action you have to take is likely to be serious.

Grievance interviews

When someone comes to you with a grievance, it is only fair to them to arrange to see them in an atmosphere which engenders trust and openness. This means holding an interview with the person in private and ensuring you are not interrupted. In many cases, the person has come to you as a last resort, having failed to deal with the problem themselves. They are likely to be tense and, perhaps, aggressive, demanding instant action; they may well be emotional about what has been going on and everything they have been 'bottling up' for some time may come pouring out.

You need to listen, but not offer advice until you can establish all the facts, and you need to help the person regain their self-control so that the grievance can be discussed relatively dispassionately. This may mean suggesting a second interview in a day or two's time when they have had a chance to calm down. You should take notes of the complaint so that you can check the facts later and, if necessary, report them to someone more senior in the organization. Despite your own prejudices, you have to recognize that the grievance is very real to the person who is concerned, otherwise they would not have come to you in the first place: treat it — and them — with the gravity the situation requires.

Grievance procedures

All organizations must provide employees with details of how to go about seeking redress of any work-related grievance, apart from those governed separately under the Health and Safety at Work Act 1974, and these grievance procedures should be agreed with representatives of any trade unions concerned. The procedures should be formal, except in very small companies, and should be given to employees in writing as part of their terms and conditions of service.

INVESTIGATE

- *What grievance procedures are laid down in your organization? Are all your staff familiar with them?*

A typical grievance procedure might have three stages in which, initially, an employee can verbally report dissatisfaction with any aspect of his or her employment to an immediate supervisor who will respond within an agreed timescale (this should be as short as possible). The supervisor is then responsible for investigating the grievance and, if possible, resolving it. If this is not possible or the employee remains dissatisfied with the outcome, he or she can state the grievance, usually in writing, to a line manager or departmental manager who will respond within an agreed timescale. If the matter remains unresolved, the line manager has to take it higher up and arrange for the employee to meet with someone more senior. If all else fails, and it is always preferable that problems are resolved internally, it may be necessary to bring in an independent third party to resolve the grievance. This might be a representative of an employees' association, a specialist consultant or a panel of arbitrators recommended by ACAS.

The role of ACAS

ACAS is the main source of independent third-party assistance when grievance reaches the stage of deadlock. It offers its services free. Its staff have a wealth of experience in achieving settlements in cases of dispute and, most importantly, only settlements resulting from ACAS intervention and conciliation can include a legally binding clause. This clause states the full and final settlement and no further legal claim can be made by an employee against this settlement. This is not the case if a settlement has not involved ACAS.

ACAS cannot intervene unless both parties, employer and employee(s), agree to independent conciliation, mediation or arbitration – these are the three services ACAS provides. Conciliation involves the attempt, through discussion and negotiation, to enable the parties involved in a dispute to reach their own agreements. *Conciliators* cannot impose or even recommend settlements. ACAS operates at a local level through its seven regional offices in England and offices in Scotland and Wales: its Head Office generally conciliates in industry-wide disputes or those which have a national impact and generate widespread public concern.

Astra, the company formed to effect a management buy-out of forty-seven skill centres from the government in 1990, sought to reduce the enhanced redundancy terms in the face of an adverse business climate. As a condition of its buy-out, Astra had been committed to retaining Civil Service redundancy terms following privatization. However, its ability to continue as a viable enterprise necessitated that it review its commitment. The trade unions, the National Union of Civil and Public Servants and the Civil and Public Services Association, resisted the changes proposed by Astra which offered terms inferior to those inherited. The parties brought the dispute to ACAS where, over two meetings, a better understanding of the issues was established and overt conflict avoided through collective conciliation. (ACAS, 1991)

The Service also provides conciliation for individual grievances such as unfair dismissal, contravention of the Wages Act 1986, sex and race discrimination and cases of complaints about equal pay.

A *mediator* can, at the request of both parties, make positive recommendations about a settlement but there is no commitment that these recommendations will be accepted. As with conciliation, all parties in the dispute have to agree to refer it to mediation.

The Manchester Evening News had proposed changes in the House Agreement in the light of a deteriorating trading position which involved the employers in a dispute with the National Union of Journalists. The whole matter was referred to ACAS for mediation in accordance with the parties' procedure agreement. The mediator met the parties on three separate occasions and was able to secure agreements on some aspects of the dispute. The remaining issues were addressed in a written report to the parties and, after considering this, the parties were able to reach a mutually acceptable agreement. (ACAS, 1991)

The *arbitrator*, on the other hand, is expected to determine the final outcome and, again, this has to be agreed by both parties beforehand. An arbitrator will listen to the case and preferred outcome of each party and may choose one of these or make some alternative decision.

In cases involving disputes over the introduction of a shorter working week without increased costs, the withdrawal of special payments for weekend working following the loss of business

> from a customer and where employers felt unable to offer an annual pay claim or proposed a deferment of the implementation date, ACAS arbitrators resolved the disputes successfully. (ACAS, 1991)

If a case of grievance develops to the stage where third-party help is required, it is important that both sides agree whether they are seeking conciliation, mediation or arbitration. The alternative to any of these can be prolonged disputes, the resolution of which may prove expensive to either or both employers and employees at the end of the day.

ACAS also provides advice on a wide range of issues related to industrial relations, employment policies and organizational effectiveness in an attempt to resolve problems and grievances before disputes arise.

> A large manufacturing company seeking to introduce total quality management invited ACAS to evaluate the effectiveness of its bonus scheme for maintenance workers and to consider other changes for the future. A joint working party which included representatives from the unions was set up to examine existing pay systems. They recommended the replacement of the proposed bonus scheme by one that rewarded employees for acquiring added skills and demonstrating the flexibility to use them.

It also provides a number of publications in the form of Advisory Booklets, Advisory Handbooks and Occasional Papers, which range over subjects including job evaluation, absence, workplace communications, performance appraisal, quality circles, motivation and supervision.

Taking disciplinary action

It is unfortunate that, by association, discipline is often linked with grievance whereas the two should be considered as entirely separate activities. Employees, as you have seen, have the right to express their dissatisfaction about shortcomings and problems related to their job and working environment and should be encouraged to follow laid down grievance procedures. 'Disciplinary action' should not be considered the result of, or even connected with, any genuine grievance voiced by an employee.

As with grievance procedures, however, there is a legal obligation to provide employees with written details of disciplinary procedures within the organization. ACAS issues the 'ACAS Code of Practice No. 1: Disciplinary practice and procedures in employment' under the 1975 Employment Protection Act. Although this code of practice cannot be enforced legally, and breach of the code is not a legal offence, employers are expected to conform to the spirit of the code. If they do not, this failure will be noted in any subsequent action, such as a claim for unfair dismissal resulting from disciplinary action.

The responsibility for formulating an effective disciplinary policy lies with an organization's management but this should be done, where possible, in agreement with employees and trade unions. Any set of disciplinary procedures and rules should take into consideration what is necessary for the safe and efficient performance of work and what is needed to maintain good working relationships between employees, and between management and employees. The procedures should be in writing, specify to whom they apply, provide for matters to be dealt with quickly and indicate the disciplinary actions which may be taken. They should also specify the levels of management who have the authority to take various forms of disciplinary action; for example, immediate superiors should not normally have the power to dismiss an employee without reference to senior management.

All employees have the right to be informed of the complaints made against them and to state their case before any action is taken. They have the right to be accompanied by a trade union representative or another employee of their choice. Except in cases of 'gross misconduct', no employee should be dismissed for a first breach of discipline and no action should be taken until the case has been fully investigated. Employees have the right of appeal against any disciplinary action taken against them.

It is quite normal for even relatively junior managers to be involved in disciplinary procedures if they are being taken against an employee for whom they are responsible. It is also normal for managers who believe it is necessary for disciplinary action to be taken to be involved in the early stages of the procedure.

Depending on the organization's disciplinary procedures, managers may be involved in collecting 'evidence' of any activity which might lead to later disciplinary action. This might include details of, for example, persistent bad timekeeping, drinking alcohol on the organization's premises, disruptive or aggressive behaviour or harassment of other staff. The employee must be given a verbal warning that this behaviour, if it continues, may result in disciplinary action being taken and that this is the first stage of a formal disciplinary procedure.

At all stages leading up to disciplinary action, notes should be made of what is happening. If a case that involves dismissal goes to an industrial tribunal, there are a number of essential documents which have to be produced. These include the contract of employment, a copy of the disciplinary procedure, any record of a disciplinary investigation or disciplinary hearing and of any appeal hearing, and copies of any previous written warnings or recorded verbal warnings.

If the behaviour continues, one or two written warnings need to be given. The final written warning needs to contain a statement that, if the behaviour recurs, this will lead to specific disciplinary action which might be suspension without pay, disciplinary transfer, a fine or dismissal. With the exception of dismissal, other sanctions can only be invoked if the contract of employment with the individual permit them.

Poor handling of discipline can lead to high staff turnover, loss of morale, decreased performance and a loss of respect for managers among employees. In some organizations, managers ignore most rule-breaking because they fear the effects of taking disciplinary action; this, too, loses them respect and can affect performance.

Avoiding the necessity to take disciplinary action need not mean turning a blind eye to infringement of rules. It can be averted if managers put time and effort into ensuring employees know exactly what the rules are in the first place and understand why they have been drawn up. Every organization is required to have a basic set of rules and procedures but these may be out of date or have been drawn up without consulting employees. Some of the rules may not even apply any longer because the need for them has been removed. Although most managers do not have the power to change organizational rules, they can request additional or specific ones for their own area of responsibility, preferably with the agreement of their staff.

Rules and procedures are supposed to be given to all employees, but this often does not happen in practice. A dog-eared and fading copy may exist on a noticeboard, ignored by everyone. You need to make sure your staff know the rules and what is likely to happen if they are broken. This might mean holding training sessions or developing an employee manual or handbook; it might involve raising points regularly at staff meetings or, at least, ensuring any notice is prominently displayed where everyone can see it.

INVESTIGATE

- *How do your staff find out about your organization's rules and regulations?*

   If there is a problem which involves violation of the rules, you need to know about it as quickly as possible either through personal observation or from your supervisors. Check your facts — is the employee genuinely breaking a rule; does he or she realize this? If there does seem to be a real or potential problem, tell the employee about your concern and arrange to have a discussion about it.

At this stage, you are not invoking formal disciplinary procedures; you are trying to avoid that being necessary. You are using informal methods in an attempt to prevent the problem getting worse. In your discussion you need to find out if the employee realizes he or she is breaking organizational rules and ask them what they are going to do about it. You should point out to them the potential penalties they might incur if formal disciplinary procedures are set in motion — not as a threat but as a statement of fact. The atmosphere of this meeting should be one of trust and support rather than of criticism. Your aim is to get the employee to understand what he or she is doing wrong and for you both to agree on a solution. If this method fails and you have to invoke the procedures, accept that this is necessary not only in order to improve the situation but to maintain your own authority and credibility with your staff.

Dismissal: the termination interview

Most managers dislike having to dismiss a member of their staff with the accompanying resentment, bitterness and grief this can involve. Some avoid a termination interview by letting staff know in writing rather than in person that they are being dismissed. This is not surprising when you consider that only about 16 per cent of managers required to dismiss others have received any training in this area.

> Andrew Cracknell, creative director of the advertising agency BSB Dorland, says: 'By its nature, firing someone is a tasteless conversation. You can't have a good sacking like you can't have a good funeral.' His best tip is to fire people in their own offices. 'People usually want to be left alone, and it means they don't have to stumble through the office afterwards. More selfishly, you can end the interview when you choose.'

There are five reasons for dismissal under the Employment Protection (Consolidation) Act 1978:

- Lack of ability, skill or qualifications.
- Misconduct.
- Dishonesty.
- Genuine redundancy.
- Other statutory enactments applying to the job (e.g. if a driver lost his or her driving licence, the person could not continue to carry out the job without breaking the law).

The Act is complex and you need to be very sure that you have good reasons for fair dismissal before embarking on the process. Any employee has the right to be given a chance to improve his or her work performance or conduct, to be given a chance to explain the reasons for his or her behaviour and to exercise the right to appeal against dismissal. Proper notice, according to the employee's contract, must be given, orally and in writing.

Geraldine Bedell (1992) has some advice for managers faced with telling someone they are going to be dismissed. She suggests:

- Writing a script beforehand to which you can refer if the situation becomes too emotional and you fear you may lose control of it.
- Rehearsing your script or whatever you are going to say.
- Choosing your time – people need to take action to find other jobs quickly and Friday afternoon is not the best time.
- Taking the telephone off the hook; avoiding interruptions.
- Trying to create a one-to-one calm atmosphere.
- Explaining, but not justifying, and avoiding recriminations.
- Setting the scene briefly, then giving the news clearly.
- Ensuring you have written details of terms you are offering and that you give the other person a copy.
- Moving quickly from giving the bad news to ways in which you can offer support.
- Closing the meeting after about 10 minutes, although you may feel you should arrange a follow-up.
- Writing notes on what took place.

Managing redundancy

> A further 60,000 construction workers were expected to lose their jobs during 1992, taking the total number of job losses in the industry since the start of the recession to 300,000.

The skills of coping with the need to make staff redundant have had to be developed by today's managers during the world recession. Even companies who had previously had a policy of 'no redundancies' have found themselves faced with the unpleasant task of reducing their workforce as part of a survival strategy. This has contributed towards the new 'industry', now worth over £50 million in the UK alone, of 'outplacement' consultancy. It is also indicative of the times we live in that management textbooks written before the mid-1980s have no section on 'redundancy'; the indexes of such books show nothing between 'recruitment' and 'reinforcement'.

Under a scheme called 'Release 92', nearly 30,000 British Telecom employees have taken voluntary redundancy and 19,500 of these left the industry at the end of July 1992. Over 30,000 more job cuts are planned by the end of 1994 which would reduce the workforce from 245,000 in 1990 to 135,000. Those taking redundancy include managers, engineers, technicians, telephone operators and telephone staff. There have been some logistical difficulties, not least because the number of requests for redundancy far exceeded expectations, and some resentment over the selection process. (*The Independent on Sunday*, 23 August 1992)

Dismissal for redundancy is deemed to be fair if:

- The redundancy is genuine and is not being claimed by the employer as the reason for dismissing an incompetent employee.
- The people selected for redundancy have been chosen on the basis of agreed criteria, which may be criteria agreed within the company or in agreement with the trade union.
- There is no suitable alternative work available; the organization is required to try to find alternative work for employees rather than declare them redundant.
- Redundancy selection does not contravene the Sex Discrimination or Race Discrimination Acts.

Actual or threatened redundancy is a tremendous strain on individuals, particularly those whose age or circumstances may make it difficult or impossible for them to find work elsewhere. It is as much a blow to their pride and self-esteem as it is to their financial security. However, J. M. Smith (1989), in an analysis of male job-seekers who sought help from a major outplacement agency, showed that it is often the most able people in an organization who are most likely to be made redundant. Managers who had been made redundant scored higher on verbal intelligence tests and had a greater variety of experience than managers in general; they were also more independent and entrepreneurial. There are three possible explanations for this. First, it is the independent, self-confident and able managers who are most likely to go for a voluntary redundancy package because they have the confidence that they will be able to get another job. Second, these kinds of managers are often seen as 'troublemakers' by organizations and redundancy can be seen as a way of getting rid of potential mavericks at a time of instability. Third, in an effort to be fair to individuals, organizations may identify managers who could more easily find jobs elsewhere as being those most suitable for redundancy.

In March 1992 a survey carried out by Coopers and Lybrand Deloitte of 600 executives selected for initial interviews found that 38 per cent had already been, or were about to be, made redundant.

In legal terms, any employee who is made redundant has the right to paid time off work to look for another job or to arrange for training. There is a statutory right to redundancy pay and notice and, where alternative work is offered, the right to a trial period in the new job without jeopardizing the right to redundancy pay.

A firm of estate agents had to make a genuine redundancy but the employee was not consulted beforehand. The company only offered alternative work of a residential nature in one region. The employee was deemed to have suffered unfair dismissal due to the company's failure to consult and to undertake a proper search for alternative work.

However, most good employers offer more than the minimum legal requirement to employees facing redundancy. They may offer relatively generous 'redundancy packages', including paying for re-training as well as other financial benefits. Many offer counselling, whether from specialists in the organization or through outplacement consultants.

Ferguson in Gosport had to close its entire plant, with nearly 700 employees being made redundant. Within two weeks of the announcement of closure, the company, with the help of a firm of outplacement consultants, embarked on a counselling programme. The same level of support was given to everyone, regardless of their job status. After holding two-hour group workshops with staff in work teams, one-to-one counselling sessions were held on a voluntary basis. By the time the company closed down, one-third of the employees had found other jobs, set up in business for themselves or retired. (Crofts, 1992)

The Army is offering training and support to the wives of soldiers facing redundancy in an attempt to ensure that the family will continue to have at least one member in paid work. Courses include small business management since this is an area many ex-servicemen enter when they leave the forces. Their wives are also offered the same financial information and counselling as their husbands.

Redundancy interviewing

Not all organizations employ outplacement consultants and, as a manager, there may be occasions when you are called upon to counsel an employee who is facing redundancy. As we pointed out in Chapter 4, counselling involves active listening to what the other person has to say, encouraging them to formulate the problem and reach their own solution. This may sound rather facile during the trauma of redundancy, but some informal counselling will be better than none at all.

The person who is being made redundant is likely to be experiencing feelings of despair and lack of confidence; there may also be considerable feelings of resentment and bitterness; there will almost certainly be a great deal of anxiety about the future. Sometimes individuals react with feelings of excitement and enthusiasm at the prospect of a 'new start', however unrealistic these may be. Whatever the reaction, the person will probably find it difficult to think and plan rationally and clearly, particularly if redundancy occurs after a long working life.

Your task as a counsellor is to try to make the other person separate out his or her feelings from thinking; to try to clarify the issues he or she has to face and work on some options for the future. The redundant employee probably thinks of himself or herself as having failed in some way and it is important to stress that it is the *job*, not the individual, which is redundant. There is a great need for the person to regain confidence and self-esteem and to start thinking about themselves in a positive way by recognizing their particular strengths. The ability of the redundant employee to manage his or her own process of finding another job is directly related to the individual's level of confidence. Much of the advice given by Geraldine Bedell earlier in this chapter about termination interviews also holds good for managers who have to tell employees that they are being made redundant.

It may have been a long time since the employee applied for a job and there may be a need for advice and help over compiling a CV or in writing letters of application. Each rejection, of course, is liable to damage confidence again and the counselling process may need to be ongoing. Practice in being interviewed for a job can be valuable and this is something you can offer relatively easily.

Many outplacement counsellors have themselves been made redundant at some time and have subsequently been trained in counselling skills. Outplacement consultants operate both as 'corporate' consultants, where the organization pays for their services on behalf of its employees, or 'private' or 'retail', where they offer their services to individuals. Private outplacement consultancy may also be offered by the organization for individuals.

IBM UK Ltd were faced with making reductions in their workforce between 1990 and 1992. They offered voluntary redundancy, targeted in particular at employees in the 40−50 years age group since the company had a disproportionately large number of managers and senior professional staff in this age bracket. They offered a package called 'Career transition programme' (CTP) which included a lump-sum payment of one month's pay for each completed year of service up to a total of twenty-four years. Volunteers could opt to take a pension at the age of 50, the normal maximum age for payment being 53.

Once an employee had decided to leave IBM, he or she was allowed paid leave of absence to find another job. Outplacement services were made available and those leaving were encouraged to place their names on the Skillbase freelance register, although they were not guaranteed employment. Senior staff could also purchase their company cars.

Because IBM were targeting their redundancy not only at a particular age group but at certain groups of staff, quarterly meetings of the company's top managers were held at which major announcements were made, including which departments would qualify for the voluntary redundancy scheme, and cascade materials were provided so that everyone could be fully informed about developments. Individuals whose skills the company wished to retain were informed that they were ineligible to apply for voluntary redundancy.

By the end of 1991, 1,907 employees had accepted voluntary redundancy and IBM were within sight of their target of 2,120 at a cost of, on average, two years' pay per head which they expected to recoup within 18−20 months. With very few exceptions, the final result was both satisfying for the company and acceptable to employees; indeed, some people who were exempted from the scheme were those who felt most resentful. (Peach, 1992)

Legal and regulatory framework

Following the correct procedures for handling grievance and disciplinary action, dismissal and redundancy involves considerable knowledge of both the legal requirements in each case and of your organization's own regulations. If you do not have a Personnel Department which can handle these matters, you will need to get the hold of up-to-date information from the following:

- ACAS: *Code of Practice No. 1: Disciplinary practice and procedures in employment* (Advisory, Conciliation and Arbitration Service, published by HMSO and available through government bookshops).

- ACAS: *Notes on disciplinary practice and procedures* (to accompany the above Code).
- ACAS: *Discipline at Work*.
- *Redundancy Handling*, ACAS booklet No. 12.

The relevant Acts mentioned in this chapter are:

- Employment Protection Act 1975
- Employment Protection (Consolidation) Act 1978
- Sex Discrimination Acts 1975 and 1986
- Race Relations Act 1976
- Equal Pay Act 1970 and Equal Pay (Amendment) Regulations 1983
- Wagest Act 1986

Summary

Employees have the right to express genuine grievances and to expect that these will be considered and resolved. Every organization is required to let employees know the procedures for reporting grievances and how they will be handled. As a manager, you are likely to be first in line when grievances are made: you need to discover the real cause of the grievance rather than try to solve an individual problem.

Grievance procedures are drawn up so that they can be followed and typically involve several stages, including the expression of grievance verbally and in writing if it remains unresolved. As the grievance continues, so it needs to be expressed higher up in the organization. If it cannot be resolved satisfactorily within the organization itself, an independent third party, such as can be provided by ACAS, can be brought in with the agreement of all parties concerned, to conciliate, mediate or arbitrate over the dispute.

Employers also have a legal obligation to provide written details of disciplinary procedures, including the penalties which may be incurred in cases of disciplinary action. All stages leading to disciplinary action need to be well-documented, particularly if it results in the dismissal of an employee. Managers need to recognize that taking disciplinary action when necessary should not be avoided: loss of respect for the manager and loss of morale in employees can both result from lack of action.

Any dismissal needs sensitive handling and requires consideration for the person concerned. It is not an enjoyable part of the job and can cause managers as much stress as the person being dismissed.

The final part of this chapter dealt with the increasing volume of redundancy in today's economic climate. Although it is difficult, if not impossible, for organizations to avoid having to make people redundant, there are ways in which support can be provided for employees who lose their jobs. These include outplacement counselling, help with finding new employment and generous redundancy packages.

Activities

There are no specific activities related to this chapter. Instead, we suggest you take some time to familiarize yourself with:

1 Your organization's grievance procedures.

2 Your organization's disciplinary procedures.

3 The relevant legislation governing grievance, disciplinary action and redundancy.

References

ACAS (1991) *Annual Report*. Advisory, Conciliation and Arbitration Service, London

Bedell, G. (1992) 'You're fired!' *The Independent on Sunday*, 31 May, p. 18

Bouwen, R. and Salipante, P. F. (1990) Behavioural analysis of grievances: episodes, actions and outcomes. *Employee Relations (UK)*, **12**(4), 27–32

Crofts, P. (1992) Outplacement: a way of never having to say you're sorry?, *Personnel Management*, May, pp. 46–50

International Labour Organization (1965) International Labour Conference Report 7 (1): Examination of Grievances and Communications within the Undertaking, ILO, Geneva, pp. 7–9

Peach, L. (1992) Parting by mutual agreement: IBM's transition to manpower cuts. *Personnel Management*, March, pp. 40–3

Smith, J. M. (1989) *Job Loss – the paradoxes of talent*, Coutts Career Consultants Ltd, Occasional Papers

Smith, P. C. (1967) The development of a method of measuring job satisfaction. *Studies in Personnel and Industrial Psychology* (ed. E. A. Fleishman), Dorset Press

Thomson, A. W. J. and Murray, V. V. (1976) *Grievance Procedures*, Saxon House/ Lexington Books, Farnborough (UK)/Lexington, Mass., pp. 17–18

Further reading

Any of the publications provided by ACAS will help you in the areas of managing adversity.

Farnham, D. (1993) *Employee Relations*, Institute of Personnel Management, London (forthcoming)

Jackson, M. (1991) *An Introduction to Industrial Relations*, Routledge, London

Marlow, J. (1991) *Industrial Tribunals and Appeals*, Bedford Square Press, London

Morin, W. J. and Carbrera, J. C. (1991) *Parting Company*, Harvest/HBJ (US)

9 Improving job satisfaction

A large part of your time as a manager is involved in planning, allocating and evaluating work carried out by your subordinates or members of your team. This is a far more complex and sensitive process than many people realize.

First you have to consider the demands of the specific job and the individual and component tasks it actually entails. Having done this, you need to take into account the requirements of the person performing that job — the skills and abilities that person will need as a minimum to achieve the expected level of performance. If, as we suggested in Chapter 2, you have carried out a Human Resource Audit, you will already have this information; if this is still low down on your list of priorities, you should aim to bring it further up, particularly if you are experiencing any symptoms of low job satisfaction in your area of responsibility. As you saw in Chapter 4, dissatisfaction with work can be a major source of absenteeism, sickness, lateness and low morale.

In this chapter we will be considering:

- The potential benefits of well-designed jobs.
- The characteristics of a well-designed job.
- Designing or redesigning the jobs of your subordinates.
- Alternative methods of organizing work.

Management in practice

The potential benefits of well-designed jobs

Much of the early work on designing jobs was undertaken in the 1970s by companies such as Saab, United Biscuits and ICI who were pioneers in experimenting with job redesign and work reorganization. Although these organizations aimed at improving job satisfaction, their 'hidden agenda' was to improve productivity. However, as Herzberg (1968) proved, increased job satisfaction will not always result in increased performance. There are other, related factors such as appropriate reward systems to be considered.

By increasing job satisfaction, however, there are a number of advantages to the organization, to the manager and to the individual employee as set out in the Figure 9.1.

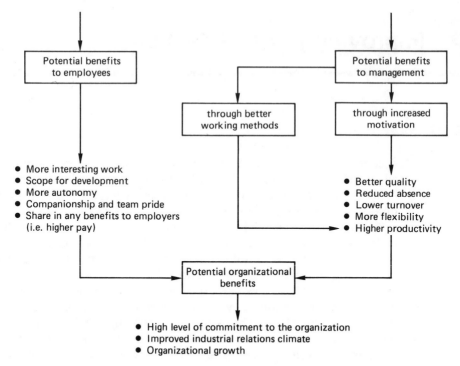

Figure 9.1 Improving job design and work organization to meet individual needs (*The Effective Manager*, Book 4, Open University, 1990)

Organizational benefits

When employees are satisfied with the work they are doing and with the work environment, they identify more closely with the employing organization. Organizations cannot buy loyalty yet they constantly wish to foster it. Employees who are committed to the organization are likely to work harder towards organizational goals, seize opportunities and new ideas and act as good public relations officers for their employers. There is less chance of industrial unrest since employees have little dissatisfaction and the organization as a whole can expect to survive and grow.

Management benefits

With highly motivated staff, managers can expect better quality performance than from subordinates who are dissatisfied with the work they are doing. The symptoms of dissatisfaction, such as absenteeism and illness, will not be present and they are likely to discover that staff are more willing and able to perform a range of jobs if their individual skills and abilities are fully developed. In turn, this should lead to improved productivity and better quality service.

Individual benefits

If a person with particular skills and abilities finds his or her job suited to those qualities, the work they are doing will be more interesting and, thus, less likely to produce stress. Repetitive and boring work is, in fact, highly stressful, particularly if it involves little opportunity for moving about. The job should have some scope for development of the individual so that he or she can see opportunities for improvement and advancement. With more control over the work, the individual has an increased sense of autonomy and freedom as to the way in which it can be carried out.

As discussed in Chapter 6, teams are more or less effective depending on a number of factors such as size, leadership and the task they are performing. But team membership also satisfies the social needs of individuals and a team which is working well engenders pride and team spirit in its members as well as providing social companionship. There may also be financial benefits from well-designed jobs if the organization shares any profits from improved performance with its employees.

However, these are *potential* benefits and you should not expect, just by re-designing a job, that all of them will naturally occur. There are, as usual, a number of other factors to be considered such as the expectations and abilities of individuals, the kind of organization in which you work and its reward systems and, finally, the kind of work which has to be performed. Although we will be looking at alternative ways of performing jobs later in this chapter, most of us work under certain constraints, not least the expectations and demands of our bosses, customers or clients.

Characteristics of a well-designed job

The early experiments on job design in the 1970s were not particularly successful for a number of reasons. The first concerned organizational constraints which remained unchallenged and, thus, existing jobs could only be partially redesigned to fit in with organizational norms. Often, because they were experimental, only certain parts of the organization benefited from selection for the redesign project; as a result, this led to tension between different areas within the same organization. But at least these schemes were a start and they generated a general determination to improve work organization and the working environment, particularly when it was possible to combine job design with the design of a new organization or where new technology was being introduced.

The main work on job design was carried out in the 1970s by Hackman and Oldham (1976), who developed a set of five core job dimensions or job characteristics; these were the essential ingredients of a well-designed job and, in an ideal situation, all five should be present. If they were, Hackman and Oldham argued, the individual would feel the job was meaningful, would have a sense of personal responsibility for the outcomes of the job and would, through feedback on performance, be personally strengthened and motivated to improve. The overall result would be high quality work performance, high internal work motivation and satisfaction for the individual and reduced absenteeism and staff turnover.

Hackman and Oldham's core job characteristics consisted of:

- Skill variety
- Task identity
- Task significance
- Autonomy
- Feedback

Skill variety

This characteristic refers to the extent to which a job requires a variety of activities so that the individual can use a number of different skills and talents. Not everyone enjoys jobs with a high degree of variety, however; some people prefer a more routinized job with which they feel 'safe' and able to cope. Others prefer as wide a variety as possible, providing they have the skills to undertake these or can be provided with necessary training and development.

Task identity

Some jobs are less satisfying than others because, not only do they use few of the jobholder's skills and abilities, but the job itself forms only a small part of a whole. The person doing the job cannot see its outcome in concrete terms. Assembly-line work, where an operator is only responsible for a small task such as welding together two pieces of metal or screwing several nuts on to passing bolts, has little task identity unless the person can see their part in the final outcome. Experiments with changing from an assembly line production method to one where each person puts together a whole or a major part of the finished product have been very successful in increasing job satisfaction – and output. Individuals become responsible for overall quality as well as the manual tasks involved.

Task significance

How important is your job to the organization? Or mine? Or the job of one of your subordinates? How 'good' do they feel about the jobs they are doing? Task significance relates to the extent to which the job has a substantial impact on the lives and work of other people either within the work environment or outside it. People who work for voluntary organizations such as Oxfam, for example, and are unwaged, are usually highly motivated because they feel that the work they are doing has a significant impact on others who are less fortunate than themselves. Hackman and Oldham cite the example of people who tighten nuts on aircraft brake assemblies; they are likely to see their work as more meaningful in terms of the overall safety of the aeroplane, its crew and passengers than someone who fills small boxes with paperclips even though the skill levels are similar.

The significance of the job will, again, depend on the individual's personal values which is why some people choose to work for Oxfam, or teach children with learning difficulties or take up nursing while others elect to program computers, drive long-distance lorries or sell designer clothes. In each case, it is the extent to which the person is satisfied by the task that he or she is doing that is important.

INVESTIGATE

- *To what extent does your own job have skill variety, task identity and task significance?*

It is possible, according to Hackman and Oldham, for one of the above factors to be missing and for the job still to be satisfying.

Autonomy

Autonomy refers to the amount of freedom and discretion the individual can exercise over the job. A job with high autonomy is likely to engender a sense of responsibility – which Herzberg (1968) identified as being one of the main elements affecting job satisfaction – providing that person wants and can cope with this. Some people prefer jobs with a low level of responsibility where they are told what to do and work to a strict schedule; this is particularly true when people have a highly complex and demanding life outside work, leaving them little energy or desire to take on additional responsibility in their jobs. However, they are not likely to be high-achievers.

Dinah noticed that her new secretary, who had seemed very keen on the job at first, was performing less and less well as time went on. She was making mistakes in simple letters, had been abrupt on the telephone with several of the senior consultants, took long lunch 'hours' and had been off sick for a day or two at a time on several occasions. On taking her to task about all this, Dinah discovered that the woman was bored with the job. 'There's lots of things I could do which you do yourself,' she complained, 'for example, you don't need to dictate every letter — just tell me what you want to say and I'll compose it. And I can organize your diary for you so that you don't book two meetings at the same time — I get the blame for that anyway. I can set up your meetings as well, and contact the other people.'

INVESTIGATE

● *How much freedom over the way they do their jobs do you give your subordinates? Could you give them more responsibility — more autonomy over what they do?*

Feedback

People need to know whether they are performing their jobs satisfactorily; they need praise for doing things well and they need help and advice if they are not performing up to standard. The advice given in Chapter 7 on giving constructive feedback is important in all aspects of the job. This may — and usually should — involve you in giving individual feedback to your staff, but other performance measures such as quality checks, formal appraisal and performance reviews can be used for this purpose. However, praise and or criticism should, ideally, be given as close to the event as possible. It is not much use saying 'By the way, you did a really good job on that account' six months after it happened, particularly to a new employee. The person might have experienced a sense of intrinsic achievement in doing a good job; how much better that sense of achievement would have been if it had had someone else's recognition.

Although Hackman and Oldham's job characteristics were developed twenty years ago, they are still recognized as being of value today. Unfortunately, not enough jobs contain all the characteristics and there is nearly always room for improvement.

Simon was working as an Administrative Officer in the Personnel Services Department of the Civil Service. He had travelled round the world extensively before deciding to settle in London and find a job. His job involved assisting in the recruitment of all grades and preparing papers for recruitment and selection Boards as well as assisting the Personnel Officer in ensuring all aspects of the payroll were submitted to the computer centre. He also had some limited responsibility for processing Service benefits and for checking computer printouts from the computer centre as well as dealing with some central staff record-keeping.

Initially, he was glad to get any job, but, as time went on, he felt frustrated that he was working well below his potential. The Personnel Officer was always checking on everything he did, even insisting on signing the letters Simon wrote regarding enquiries from staff and public and he never seemed to have a job from start to finish − it was always bits of jobs. Although he had a fairly clear idea of the career structure in the Civil Service, and how low down he was in it, he had no idea whether he was performing up to or below standard. Finally he demanded an interview with the Personnel Officer.

The interview did not start well, as Simon was frustrated and fed up with the job which made him defensive and critical. Fortunately, the Personnel Officer thought highly of him, although she had never told him this, and badly wanted to keep him. She explained that she always checked on new staff over the first eighteen months but admitted that Simon was now perfectly competent to sign his own letters and, indeed, to take on more responsibility. After a training course, he would serve on selection Boards himself and could delegate some of the routine paperwork; he could therefore take charge of the whole recruitment process from placing an advertisement to participating in the selection of candidates. This would certainly increase Simon's autonomy and the identity and significance of that particular task. He would also set up his own quality control system to check on the effectiveness of his recruitment and selection process and she promised to review this with him every three months.

Designing or redesigning the jobs of your staff

Very few of us get the chance to design jobs from scratch; sometimes you may be lucky enough to be involved in drawing up job descriptions or specifications for new jobs created as a result of growth or the introduction of new technology. And, of course, you can use the opportunity created by recruitment to redefine an existing job.

Designing the job itself is one part of the process; the other is matching the right person to the right job so that the degree of skill variety, task identity and task significance matches the needs and abilities of the individual. There are, however, a number of ways in which some of the characteristics identified by Hackman and Oldham can be improved, including:

- job rotation (increasing skill variety);
- job enrichment (increasing responsibility and thus task identity and significance and autonomy);
- autonomous working groups (increasing autonomy);
- quality circles (increasing job satisfaction).

Job rotation

Many organizations still subscribe to the concept of 'job specialization', based on the ideas of Adam Smith and Frederick Taylor (1856–1917). Taylorism or the principles of 'scientific management' were developed by Taylor in the nineteenth century by applying 'scientific' rules to management. He believed that 'The principal object of management should be to secure the maximum prosperity of the employer, coupled with the maximum prosperity of each employee' (Taylor, 1947).

INVESTIGATE

- *Do you consider this to be the 'principal object of management'?*

Although the principle seemed laudable, the method was less effective than the ideal. Taylor recommended what later developed into work study programmes, breaking down a job into its component tasks and defining a set rate of pay for standard performance. In order to achieve this standard performance, he recommended that employees would need to be 'standardized', scientifically selected and trained. The principles involved systematic observation and measurement of both the job and the jobholder and maximum specialization was emphasized.

The problem with this approach was that it appeared to reduce the human element to the level of machines, but Taylor argued that his ideas were misunderstood and that employers only followed those principles which suited their own ends; they did not, for example, subscribe to his insistence that there should be no limit to the earnings of high-producing workers (Pugh and Hickson, 1989).

A high degree of specialization, however, conflicts with Hackman and Oldham's idea of skill variety, and job rotation is one way of increasing this. It is a form of internal job transfer to enable employees to gain a wider understanding of the work of the organization and to use different skills and competence. It reduces the boredom and monotony associated with repetitive, low-level tasks but its benefits are limited in contributing significantly towards increasing job satisfaction.

Job enrichment

> A report for the Chemical Industries Association showed that
> working practices in 1991 were becoming more flexible. Job
> enrichment was becoming increasingly common where operators
> were not only performing the job for which they had been originally
> trained, but were undertaking routine maintenance and other
> tasks which developed other skills.

Job enrichment (sometimes called job enhancement) is a form of
increasing satisfaction recommended by Herzberg (1968) providing
it is aimed specifically at increasing the level of responsibility of the
individual. It must not be confused with 'job enlargement' which
too often means just giving the employee more work of the same
type. According to Herzberg, the following principles of job enrichment can improve motivation:

1 The manager removes some controls while retaining some of the
   accountability (increases individual responsibility and sense of
   personal achievement).
2 The manager increases the accountability of individuals for their own
   work (increases individual responsibility and provides recognition).
3 The manager gives the person a complete natural unit of work for
   which he or she is accountable (increases responsibility and sense
   of achievement and provides recognition).
4 The manager grants additional authority to an employee in his or
   her work (increases responsibility and a sense of achievement,
   provides recognition and additional autonomy).
5 The manager periodically gives feedback to the employee (increases
   feedback and provides recognition).
6 The manager introduces new and more difficult tasks into the job
   not previously handled by the jobholder (provides opportunities for
   personal growth and learning).
7 The manager assigns individuals specific or specialized tasks,
   enabling them to become experts (increases responsibility and
   provides opportunities for personal growth and learning).

Providing job enrichment is not simple, but it can be very effective.
The first step is to select jobs in which it is relatively easy to make
changes within existing constraints, in which job satisfaction appears
to be low and in which increased motivation is likely to improve
performance. Assume these jobs can be changed — avoid being
hidebound by organizational tradition and the statement 'but we've
always done it this way'.

Think of ways in which the jobs might be enriched without

getting involved in the practicalities at this stage, but make the options practical in the sense of real actions. Select some of the ideas for further consideration and try them out on a small group of employees. Evaluate the differences the changes make in performance over time — you should expect performance to improve immediately, then drop before rising again to a steady rate.

Production workers at GM's Delco-Remy Plant in Fitzgerald, Georgia have jobs that are unlike those in most manufacturing companies. They prepare budgets, help determine staffing levels, keep track of their own timesheets, are entirely responsible for plant safety, generate requirements for new equipment, carry out all maintenance and minor repairs on machines and perform their own quality checks. (Described in Peters, 1988)

International Computers Ltd (ICL) decided to automate the majority of its circuit board assembly production at its Kidsgrove plant but without the attendant problems associated with assembly line work. Employees who had previously been responsible for assembling circuit boards manually were retrained and given additional responsibility for maintenance, minor repairs and quality control. Employees welcomed the opportunity to acquire new skills and, in particular, the increased level of responsibility the new jobs provided.

Autonomous working groups

Increased responsibility and autonomy can also be provided by teamworking where the team is responsible for work allocation and organization. The construction industry is a good example of this where work is sub-contracted to teams of workers. These working groups can also provide opportunities for increased skill variety and opportunities for more flexible working and individual development. Additionally, they provide social companionship and a sense of pride in the team's work. Not all teams are effective, however, and conflict may arise between team members, particularly if there is individual competition for different tasks; there is also the need for team leaders to be trained in the skills of leadership and supervision if they are to take over the duties of work organization.

Quality circles

The introduction of the ideas of Total Quality Management and programmes of continuous quality improvement have brought with them a commitment to employee involvement in all aspects of quality, including the setting up of 'quality circles'. These circles are usually set up to tackle a particular project where quality improvement is necessary.

To be successful, quality improvement programmes need commitment from top management; this means not only looking at quality control systems and rewarding individuals and teams for improved quality, but actively encouraging participation through providing time and training.

Bill worked in the Development Services Department of ICL. With his colleagues, he formed a quality circle to tackle problems associated with their work. In this case, it involved the transportation and handling of small electronic components. The group were given time off to hold their meetings and a room in which to meet. Their success in solving the problem was rewarded by a cheque for £1,000. Bill himself felt he had benefited from the project by learning more about working with and managing other people in the quality circle.

Quality circles are more successful when they are coping with issues that affect the jobs of their members rather than with more general and ambiguous problems. They can contribute to job satisfaction through the sense of achievement their members feel when quality is improved and through recognition of their work.

INVESTIGATE

● *Could any of the above ideas be put into practice in your area of responsibility to increase job satisfaction?*

Alternative methods of organizing work

Since the traditional 'job for life' concept has virtually disappeared and the widespread introduction of new technology has had a major impact on job design, there is an increasing opportunity to survey normal working practices and see whether these could be changed.

> A recent survey of 250 leading businesses, including Rank Xerox
> and Pacific Bell, found productivity gains of up to 60 per cent with
> an average increase of 45 per cent among staff who worked from
> home. It is now believed that one office worker in two could work
> from home if provided with a fax machine and computer modem
> to receive and transmit work. If only 15 per cent of workers
> operated from home, £5.5 billion would be wiped off the national
> office rent bill and the nation would save £1.9 billion on fuel.
> Commuting problems would recede. Estimates suggest that
> 625,000 people, mainly self-employed, work from home. This
> figure is expected to rise to around 3.3 million by the mid-1990s.
> (Report in the *Guardian*, 17 June 1992)

Flexible working hours, jobsharing, homeworking, adaptation of
work methods for people with disabilities are some of the more
enterprising ways of work organization. They are not without their
problems nor, in some cases, without high initial costs, but they can
all bring benefits if well managed.

Flexible working hours

Many organizations already operate embryonic flexible working
hours but few have looked into all the opportunities which are
available. Flexibility in working arrangements is attractive to
employees and can contribute significantly to job satisfaction. The
organization can benefit from lower absenteeism, better timekeeping,
reduced staff turnover, higher work commitment and improved
performance; employees see the advantages of more leisure time,
less time spent commuting at peak times, increased responsibility
and the ability to schedule work and personal life to the individual's
satisfaction.

Flexible working hours can range from a daily, fixed-but-flexible
starting and finishing time to the working day to a system of
annualized hours over a full year. Employees may work any eight
consecutive hours, for example, between 7.30 a.m. and 6.30 p.m.
This has the added advantage in providing maximum cover for
essential operations such as telephone enquiries or emergencies
over a longer period than the typical 9–5 working day. Or they may
work a given number of hours during a working week or fortnight,
some of which is designated as 'core time' (when staff are required
to be at their place of work) and the rest as 'flexible time'. This
flexible time might account, for example, for four hours of any
working day; in agreement with the manager, the employee can
select which particular four hours he or she will work for the rest of
each day.

Strathkelvin District Council in Glasgow introduced annual hours into its leisure centres in 1991. The system was designed to match consumer usage of leisure centres and swimming pools which fluctuates over the week and the month. Contracts are for around 1,750 hours annually, including around 40 and 80 reserve hours when staff can be called in on at least one week's notice to help with events such as swimming galas or to cover for sickness. The rota of hours to be worked by each employee is drawn up a year in advance to enable people to schedule their leisure time.

Strathkelvin encountered some resistance initially with the GMB general union and amended their original proposals before implementing the scheme.

Express Foods, based in Shropshire, introduced annual hours in 1989 with considerable success and with support from the union. Rotas for the 1,792-hour working year are agreed more than a year ahead and a 'super-crew' of four highly paid and highly skilled individuals are on call to cover emergencies. The workforce are happy to work over weekends when it means larger blocks of days off during the week.

However, annualized hours systems involve a great deal of management time to set up, agree and implement. One of its undoubted benefits is the ability to roster employees to work more and longer hours during peak times and fewer, shorter hours during slack periods.

Compressed working week

This arrangement allows employees to work longer than normal hours for part of a week and have the rest of the time free. It is another variation of flexible working hours but can result in increased fatigue at work, concern and resistance from unions and increases the chance of employees taking on 'second jobs' during their free time, thus reducing commitment and increasing fatigue.

Jobsharing

With jobsharing, two part-time employees split one full-time job; the salary and hours of work are usually split equally but there is also room for unequal shares. This can benefit people with childcare or other dependant commitments, people who tire easily or have physical limitations, people who want to indulge in part-time study and older people who want to phase in their retirement. Providing the two jobsharers communicate fully with each other, this arrangement can work well, but continuity is essential.

Career-break schemes

Although not defined as an alternative working method, organizations which make provisions for employees to take career breaks while retaining their right to return to work at a later date, usually benefit from such schemes. They are normally aimed at women or men who want to take time at home to be with young children but they can also be used for employees who want time off to study full-time or to experience working practice elsewhere.

> Barclays Bank have experienced a big increase in the number of women returning to work after maternity leave after introducing its career-break scheme. There is now an option open to women in senior grades to take a long break or return to work part-time for a period of two years in their existing grade. Providing they work at least 14 hours a week, part-time women in the scheme continue to receive pro rata all the benefits of full-time work, including pensions. Since the scheme was introduced in 1988, Barclays has increased its retention of women workers by one-third.

> Several companies, particularly in Scandinavia and other parts of mainland Europe, operate local childminding schemes which enable women to return to work. In the UK, Allied Dunbar, Glaxo and East Sussex County Council are among organizations which offer this service. It involves setting up a network of trained childminders and, in some cases, providing the necessary training, who are then matched with employees who wish to take advantage of the scheme.

With the need to recruit and retain more women in the workforce, career-break schemes make good sense to enterprising employers.

Working from home

Although considerable potential savings in rents, heat, lighting and travel could be made if more people worked from home, this is still regarded with suspicion by many employers. There is a feeling of lack of control — but it may merely be a lack of trust in subordinates. Advances in technology and reductions in its cost make it a sensible option to consider.

Oxfordshire County Council have introduced a 'flexiplace' project which gives staff greater flexibility over where and when they work. For example, Jan, a management accountant, works 10 hours of her 30-hour week at home. Office time is used for meetings and face-to-face communication; at home, she works on spreadsheets on her computer. This fits in well with her home commitments; she tries to work in the office during school hours and at home in the evening. In this way, she can spend a satisfying amount of time each day with her family. Alice, whose job as an Education Adviser involves considerable travelling around the County, has a child of school age but opts to work from home most of the time even though her daughter does not require home based childcare: she goes into the office for meetings but finds it easier to fit in her other commitments by travelling to and from her home.

Jobs that involve a great deal of computer-based work can readily be done from home. Employers provide fax machines, mobile phones, answering machines, pagers and laptop computers needed for home-based employees to keep in touch with colleagues and clients. People whose work involves a lot of travelling such as social workers and sales staff can also use their home as a base rather than take up office space which is left empty most of the time.

IBM sales staff and others who spend much of their time away from the workplace are now provided with mobile telephones and laptop computers in the creation of the 'deskless office'. In the workplace, desks are shared between two or more employees who work in sales, client support, servicing and engineering in IBM's London and Glasgow offices. A similar system is operated in the offices of Coopers and Lybrand Deloitte whereby consultants who need to work in the office when they are not out meeting clients are allocated part of a filing cabinet. They work at any available desk, letting the switchboard know on which telephone extension they can be reached that day.

Not everyone wants to work from or at home. Many people enjoy the social life they find at work and not all home environments are suitable for working in. The loss of social interaction, 'corridor conversations' and knowing what is going on can lower an employee's interest in and commitment to the organization.

Increasing opportunities for people with disabilities

There are about 6 million people with disabilities in the UK, 2.4 million of whom are of working age and, of these, 31 per cent are currently in paid work. Many of those not in work are barred by lack of physical access to offices or workplaces by the failure of employers to recognize and value the person rather than the manifestation of his or her physical disability.

The introduction of the Americans with Disabilities Act in the USA has highlighted the prejudices and assumptions which create barriers to the employment of people with physical disabilities. Employers tend to believe that to employ someone with a disability means having to make costly changes to machinery or premises such as providing lifts or ramps for wheelchair access or a braille keyboard for blind operators. In fact, where there is an initial cost, this is often offset by the commitment to work of the person who is disabled.

The American company Frisch is a restaurant chain with the motto 'We look after the people who look after us'. It has built up a reputation for being a family firm, running family restaurants and treating its employees as members of one big happy family.

With the introduction in 1992 of the Americans with Disabilities Act, there has been considerable pressure, and cost, for organizations to adapt their working environment to make 'reasonable accommodation' for anyone covered by the Act to perform 'the essential functions of the job'. Frisch were well ahead of the Act.

Turnover in the restaurant business is high; in 1989, turnover at Frisch's was 260 per cent, reduced to 230 per cent by 1991. The company operates 'Project Opportunity' aimed at recruiting people with disabilities, with a target of 200 in a workforce of 7,000. To help to accommodate people with disabilities, Frisch provides special aids or amends the job itself as necessary; they have also introduced jobsharing. In the light of demographic trends and growing pressure for similar legislation in Europe, other countries will have to take a proactive approach. (Pickard, 1991b)

Summary

Changing the design of certain jobs can increase job satisfaction and benefit the individual, management and the organization as a whole. Well-designed jobs are characterized by the amount of skill variety, task identity, task significance, autonomy and feedback they involve.

There are a number of ways in which existing jobs can be made more satisfying through redesign. These include job rotation, job enrichment and the creation of autonomous working groups and quality circles. Each of these methods can be used to increase one or more of the characteristics of well-designed jobs.

Another way of reorganizing work is to consider changes in working hours and practices. Changes can include the introduction of flexible working hours, jobsharing, homeworking and adaptation of work methods for people with disabilities. Organizations that have introduced changes like these have not only found that job satisfaction has increased but that they have widened the scope of their recruitment net, reduced staff turnover and absenteeism and provided greater opportunities for work among some minority groups.

| **Activities** |

1

Which of the following ways of improving job satisfaction for your subordinates might you be able to introduce:
- job rotation;
- job enrichment;
- increasing the autonomy of working groups;
- creating quality circles within an overall policy of continuous quality improvement?

2

When did you last give informal feedback to a subordinate on his or her performance?

3

Which jobs, currently carried out by people without disabilities, could be adapted for people with disabilities?

4

Which of the jobs in your area of responsibility could be adapted to:
- flexible working hours;
- compressed working week;
- job sharing;
- partial or complete home-based work;
- performance by someone who is disabled?

5

What advantages and disadvantages can you see in introducing any of the changes you have selected in (1), (3) and (4) above?

References

Hackman, J. R. and Oldham, G. R. (1976) Motivation through the design of work: test of a theory. *Organisational Behaviour and Human Performance*, **16**, 250–79

Herzberg, F. (1968) One more time: how do you motivate employees? *Harvard Business Review*, **46**, 53–62

Peters, T. (1988) *Thriving on Chaos*, Knopf, New York, pp. 290–1

Pickard, J. (1991a) Annual hours: a year of living dangerously? *Personnel Management*, August, pp. 38–43

Pickard, J. (1991b) Catering for people with disabilities. *PM Plus*, November, pp. 20–1

Pugh, D. S. and Hickson, D. J. (1989) *Writers on Organisations*, Penguin, Harmondsworth

Taylor, F. W. (1947) *Scientific Management*, Harper and Row, London

Further reading

Many of the books recommended in Chapter 4 are also related to the improvement of job satisfaction. *Work versus family?* (1991), produced by the Dawlish Hall Educational Foundation, and the ACAS Occasional Papers 'Quality circles – a broader perspective' and 'Self-regulating work groups' are useful.

10 Managing change through people

Introduction

'In today's increasingly uncertain, competitive and fast-moving world, companies must rely more and more on individuals to come up with new ideas, to develop creative responses and push for changes before opportunities disappear or minor irritants turn into catastrophes. Innovations, whether in products, market strategies, technological processes or work practices, are designed not by machines but by people.' (Moss Kanter, 1992)

'Organizations are never static: something about them is always changing. For example, there is turnover in the membership, new administrative procedures are introduced, or a new customer arrives on the scene. None of these events is completely self-contained; each has implications for other aspects of organizational life. Some of them obviously result from decisions made within the organization, some of them originate with decisions outside, and others just seem to happen. The common factor is that when something changes, whether or not it has been planned or decided by organizational members, it will have repercussive effects which will be variously welcomed, discarded or ignored by people within and outside the organization. Their reactions will in turn affect other things.' (Dawson, 1992)

Most of this book has been about managing change of one sort or another – recruiting new staff, managing changes in individual and group behaviour, managing the changing processes which teams go through, managing people's development, coping with changes in people's working lives, looking at innovative ways in which people's jobs can be changed and improved. Writers on organizational change see it as essential if organizations and the people who work in them are to grow and develop or even keep up with the competition: the media are full of stories of change.

> '... a worldwide recession, characterized by business failures and the challenge of turnarounds. In the United Kingdom, a Conservative government has imposed new goals on both public and private sectors of the economy. To this must be added the explosion of information technology. The combination is presenting all organizations, large and small, with formidable challenges of change.' (Mayon-White, 1986)

As a manager, you have a choice. The choice is not between managing change or not managing change but between managing change through people or despite people. In virtually every case, the former is more successful.

Although some people see change as a challenge and an opportunity, others fear it. They see change as threatening because organizational change, however small, usually involves people in changing their existing working practices and processes and even their attitudes towards the job and others in the organization.

Your role in change will depend on your role in the organization. For junior or first-line managers, change is often imposed from higher up in the organization and they have to manage the process; for more senior managers, there is the opportunity to contribute to the planning of change.

In this chapter, we include:

- Pressures for change.
- Levels of change.
- Stages of change.
- Responses to change.

Management in practice

Pressures for change

Pressures for change usually come from outside the organization in the first place, from changes in the organization's environment. These external pressures can combine with pressures from inside the organization, such as the need to increase productivity or improve performance or the need to improve working conditions. Although both will be considered separately here, they are nearly always interlinked.

External pressures for change

The rapidly changing environment in which organizations exist in today's world creates continuous pressure from change. These pressures can be categorized as social, technological, political, economic, environmental and market-related, as shown in Figure 10.1. However, these categories are interdependent and it is rare for change to be the result of one pressure alone.

Social pressures for change

Social pressures generate changes which are related to the way people think and act in their everyday lives. People today have different attitudes, values and expectations from their parents and grandparents; for example, they expect higher standards of hygiene and physical welfare in their domestic and working environments than past generations. People today take television, fax machines and camcorders for granted; they travel abroad regularly and experience different cultures. More women work full time while bringing up a family. There are different attitudes towards issues such as marriage and divorce, contraception, illegitimacy and the balance between working and home life.

People expect and demand more in the quality of their working life; they are less inclined to accept authority without reason from older or senior people in the organization than before. They expect a higher standard of service from both public and private providers of education, health care and leisure. People live longer and expect to be active for longer than past generations did. Because of changed attitudes towards domestic responsibilities, the birth rate has declined with the result that fewer young people are now entering the workforce.

Figure 10.1 External pressures for change

Organizations need to respond to these social pressures for change. Quite apart from legal and regulatory requirements for minimum standards of health and safety in the workplace, employers increasingly find that they have to improve working conditions in order to improve job satisfaction; with a declining, younger workforce, they need to recruit and retain more women, which brings pressure for better childcare provision. They need to increase financial and non-financial benefits and 'perks' to attract and keep their employees.

> Women on maternity leave from the Scottish Widows insurance company receive monthly bonuses to encourage them to return to work. This bonus is made up of 50 per cent of the difference between the salary they lose on maternity leave and the state maternity pay they receive and works out at about £125 per month.

> The Storehouse group has responded to pressures to recruit and retain quality employees during the recession. It is piloting a 'cafeteria' system of benefits from which employees can choose including pensions, life assurance, medical insurance, cars, disability insurance, holidays and personal financial planning.

> Digital offer their employees contractual choice which involves a choice of workplace, including homeworking, and a choice of working time.

INVESTIGATE

● *Can you think of any changes in your own organization which were a result of social pressures?*

Technological pressures

The impact of the revolution in information and communication technology in the latter part of this century has been immense. Computers and fax machines are common office equipment now, whereas in many organizations they did not exist five or ten years ago. The mobile telephone and electronic mail have made communication almost instantaneous and decreased the problem of geographical distance. Data is readily accessible on-line; filing cabinets have disappeared; meetings can be held through computer conferencing.

Among engineering companies in Sheffield 54 per cent have introduced new technology in the past three years. Most companies found that they needed more skilled employees to work with the new technology and that they did not have the capacity within the company to train existing employees: increased training costs appear to be an unexpected result of introducing new technology.

The demand for education at school level in the use of information technology has prompted the Women into Information Technology Foundation to provide 500 teachers with practical experience in this area.

Most organizations have succumbed to these technological pressures for change; otherwise, they would not survive in today's competitive environment. Computer studies are taught in schools as well as in colleges and universities – people have become used to keyboards and secretarial and clerical jobs have changed. Working practices and production processes have all been affected.

Smith Kline Beecham have developed a telephone news service based on voice mail technology and made it available to all its employees. At no charge, employees can dial the news service from home or work and select from a menu which includes share prices, industry news and a 'City' report, all of which are updated regularly.

In the field of personnel management alone, computerized systems have been introduced which can cope with absence, turnover and salary histories of employees as well as education and qualifications data, job experience, health and safety and training. There are succession planning and management development planning packages for executives and programmes which deal with all the tasks involved in internal and external recruitment such as logging vacancies and applications, producing job descriptions, vacancy lists, reports and statistical analyses. At higher levels are packages which can be used to evaluate current human resource strategies and model proposals still at the planning stage on a 'what if' basis. There are packages which scan documents into a computer and store them on an optical disc — the list is almost endless.

The Dutch airline, KLM, has a networked personnel system which covers more than fifty locations and allows their personnel department to respond to staff-related questions within, on average, five minutes.

North West Regional Health Authority use a computerized system to receive data from each health authority's personnel and pay databases which are then presented as aggregated information for senior managers.

New technology in the car industry has put pressure on European car engine manufacturers to change production methods. Machine running time can be increased which has had an impact on work flow and lead times in order to keep equipment fully utilized.

INVESTIGATE

- *In the past five years, what technological pressures for change have resulted in working practice or process changes in your organization?*

Economic pressures

Factors such as increases and decreases in unemployment, the rate of inflation, interest rates and other products of the world recession have had a profound effect on organizations. In many cases, these economic fluctuations have contributed to the survival or death of companies, particularly small and medium-sized organizations. And, when a company goes out of business, its suppliers will also be affected. Most organizations have been affected adversely by the recession, resulting in cut-backs and redundancies; the story is familiar to everyone.

Coping with economic change, particularly in the present recession, means that organizations can no longer expect stability. If its major customer goes out of business or takes its custom elsewhere or a new competitor enters the market, the organization's economic situation can plummet overnight. For managers, it means keeping a close eye on productivity and performance and, too often, having to manage redundancy or 'downsizing'.

In 1990, the level of redundancies in the service sector rose by 40 per cent with some 83,000 job losses; manufacturing suffered 69,000 redundancies. (1990 Labour Force Survey)

The finance sector has been hit badly by the recession: 24,000 jobs have already disappeared with the threat of a further 24,000 to come. By mid-1992, 550 banking and insurance outlets had closed.

Political pressures

Changes in taxation and law affect organizations. In particular, at the moment, the Single European Market has brought changes in the law affecting employment and trade and this European social action programme is likely to continue for some time. For example, UK health and safety law is undergoing its most fundamental process of change since the passing of the Health and Safety at Work Act of 1974 as a result of directives adopted by the European Community; these changes will impact significantly on employers and employees alike in all sectors.

Changes in the political leadership of the country or a local authority can also affect organizational performance. For example, the government decision to extend compulsory competitive tendering to professional and technical local authority activities has both widened their scope for providing training and increased opportunities for training. Proposals for changes in the provision and use of work equipment, which implement European directives, will apply to virtually all industrial sectors and service occupations.

INVESTIGATE

- *Can you think of any changes in working practice or in policy which have come about in your organization as a result of political pressure from outside?*

Environmental pressures

Although all external pressures could be described as 'environmental' in that they come from the environment outside the organization, the term is used here to describe pressures on organizations to take an ethical approach to their local community. This includes pollution of the land, water or air around the organization's physical sites, levels of noise, disturbance to others, consideration for other road users, rights of access and so on.

> Prince Charles has urged that community involvement should be part of mainstream management at the annual meeting of Business in the Community (BIC). BIC have produced a suggested action guide which emphasizes employee involvement in the community which, they claim, will provide opportunities for recruiting, developing and retaining skilled and motivated staff.

Apart from those which are located on industrial sites, many organizations are physically situated within communities of other users, whether in inner city or semi-rural areas. Pressure can be brought upon organizations to change working practices or processes which adversely affect people and land which surround them.

> The thirteen employees of the Bristol-based Mosaic Consultancy Group each give 5 per cent of their time, which amounts to one day a month, to working in the local community. Their involvement ranges from running local youth groups and counselling students to training people in local trusts in management skills.

> Two employees of ICI won an award from the company after they had persuaded it to set up an ecology team. Now all ICI sites have a policy to conserve and enhance wildlife in the area.

Market-related pressures

Market demand for products and services is an obvious pressure for organizations to change. Demand can rise or fall and the organization needs to react appropriately. Markets can also fluctuate as suppliers of goods or services change their pricing policies or delivery mechanisms. Five or ten years ago, the public and non-profit sectors were only peripherally involved in market demand and supply; this has all changed as public sector organizations have been forced to become more accountable and market-orientated.

The public sector example shows how interlinked external pressures for change can be. This sector has experienced all the different types of pressures described here – socially, through changes in values and expectations, technologically in the need to become more efficient, politically, through changes in legislation and funding, economically, through the requirement to become competitive and accountable and, finally, to become client- or customer-focused.

INVESTIGATE

- *Have there been any recent changes in your organization as a result of changes in market demand or supply?*

Internal pressures for change

Pressures for change from within an organization can be 'top-down' or 'bottom-up'; that is, they can come from the leader of the organization or senior management or from the organization's employees.

If you are relatively junior in your organization, you have probably experienced top-down change. Your reaction to it will have depended on how it was communicated to you, how closely it affected you personally and whether you were consulted about the change and its effects at any point. Except in times of real crisis, top-down change is usually resented by those it affects lower down in the organization.

Top-down change needs to be handled sensitively and involve as many people as possible lower down in the organization if it is going to be accepted without resistance. Channels of communication, upward and downward, need to be effective and staff need to be kept informed about plans for change. Where time and other pressures allow, as much consultation as is possible about the way the change will be implemented and its effects on individuals and groups will result in a higher rate of acceptance and even positive enthusiasm.

Radical change, whether as a result of external or internal pressures or a combination of these, often has to be imposed from the top when a Chief Executive or management team is charged with turning around a failing organization. It is a form of crisis management which has had to become more common as large and small companies have been affected by the world recession.

> In the UK, organizations such as Leyland, British Steel and ICI have experienced radical turn-arounds, involving multimillion pound investments in new technology, sales of non-productive assets and a much tougher attitude towards the selection, assessment and rewarding of employees. (Hunt, 1986)

Radical change is usually engendered by strong external pressures and the likelihood of collapse unless drastic action is taken. It usually involves large-scale redundancies or relocation of staff and will only be successful if senior management is committed to the strategy.

Pressure from staff can be very effective in creating change, providing senior management are prepared to take notice. If ignored, it can degenerate into dissatisfaction and even result in industrial action.

> Employees at Howard's Dairies had petitioned for longer rest periods for some time, but their arguments were ignored. Eventually, their grievance reached the level where the union was brought in and a long and bitter battle with the employers was fought before going to arbitration. The arbitrator found for the employees and the company was forced to increase rest times accordingly. However, since the dispute had involved the staff in working to rule over a period of several weeks, the company had lost several major customers during this time and its financial outlook was bleak.

> The issue of passive smoking and its effect on the health of employees who do not smoke themselves has led to considerable pressure from non-smokers. Many organizations are adopting policies in response to employee demands.

With all these pressures on organizations to change, you would expect there to be other factors which constrain change from taking place; this, of course, is true. Factors which limit change and can prevent it from occurring could include financial or other resource constraints, people's attitudes and resistance to change and legal or other restrictions. The psychologist Kurt Lewin devised a model which has been called 'forcefield analysis' as a way of looking at change situations (Figure 10.2).

Pressures for change, Lewin called 'driving forces'; these included any external or internal pressures but might also include individuals

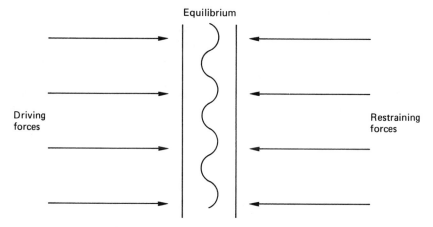

Figure 10.2 Forcefield analysis (adapted from Lewin, 1951)

or groups of people. 'Restraining forces' are Lewin's term for factors which are preventing change from taking place and these too can include individuals or groups. When the driving and restraining forces for change are equal, then a state of equilibrium exists — in other words, nothing happens. If the relative strengths of either the driving or restraining forces change, then there is activity, which may consist either of change or of a deeper entrenchment into preserving the status quo. By varying the width of the arrows representing the forces, as in Figure 10.3, relative strengths can be assessed. In any situation, each of the arrows would have a title that described the individual driving or restraining force.

You need to identify the driving and restraining forces of any change you are proposing to make in order to analyse how success-ful — or otherwise — it may be. If you find that the restraining

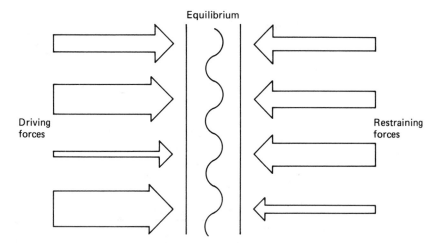

Figure 10.3 Assessing the relative strengths of driving and restraining forces

forces are equal to, or stronger than, the driving forces, you will need to strengthen the driving forces. This could be accomplished by providing more resources, financial or human, to add to the driving forces you have already identified. It could also, and often more easily, be achieved by reducing the strength of the restraining forces. You could, for example, decrease fear of change as a restraining force by involving people in the plans for change and reducing their level of anxiety about its outcome.

Levels of change

The length of time needed for managing change and the degree of difficulty you should expect are both directly related to the level of the change which is being proposed, as shown in Figure 10.4. Changes can be made at the individual, group and organizational levels and a change which affects a single individual can be expected to be simpler to manage and to take less time than one which affects groups of people or the whole organization. This is, however, rather simplistic since making a small change to the job of one individual can quite often affect others. For example, if I changed from giving work to my secretary in manuscript to dictating it, her method of work would change but the effect would probably be restricted to her alone. If, however, I asked her to work from home, such a change would involve others in supplying her with appropriate equipment, making arrangements for cover for my telephone calls when I was absent and, probably, widespread reactions from other secretarial and clerical staff concerning their working conditions; the level of the change would not be at the individual level but at the group and, even possibly, the organizational levels. A major consideration in planning change is to identify its effects at all levels before putting it into practice.

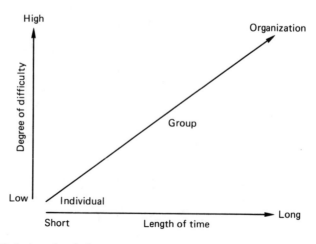

Figure 10.4 Levels of change

INVESTIGATE

- *Think of a change in which you have been involved – was it at the individual, group or organizational level?*

Stages of change

When a change is taking place, at any of the three levels described above, it needs to go through three critical stages if it is to have a chance of success. These stages, also identified by Kurt Lewin (1951), are:

- Unfreezing
- Changing
- Refreezing

Unfreezing

'Unfreezing' relates to the need to change existing attitudes towards working practices and processes before the change can begin to take place – it is the preparation stage. This is when communication about any proposed change is vital if people are to understand and support it. This may mean holding open meetings at which plans for change can be discussed by everyone concerned, or creating a newsletter to inform people, particularly those who may be involved and interested but who cannot attend meetings. It may mean holding one-to-one talks with key people and arranging for more widespread communication and reassurance on a cascade basis. If the change is going to involve people acquiring new skills, arrangements for training should fall into this stage as well. It is a time of planning and scheduling, but also of being able to alter plans in the light of consultation with other people.

Changing

This is the implementation stage, and its success will depend on the thoroughness of your planning and preparation in the first stage. In a survey of ninety-three private sector organizations where decisions, often about change, were implemented, the following conclusions were drawn:

- that the implementation stage took much longer than people expected and that timescales were often unrealistic;
- that, in many cases, major problems occurred at the stage of implementation which had not been identified at the planning stage;

- that where task forces, committees, project teams etc. were involved, co-ordination was not effective;
- that dealing with crises and problems which arose at this stage detracted from the implementation itself;
- that the skills and abilities of employees were often over-estimated;
- that not enough training and instruction were provided;
- that factors outside the organization's control, such as legal, governmental or economic changes, had an adverse effect on implementation.

Although these findings suggest that careful planning can be, and often is, overturned by unforeseen events during the second stage of change, it is usually the rigidity of plans which tends to be self-destructive in this way. If the situation changes, then so must the plan. There is a need for maximum flexibility in the planning and implementation of change, and change teams need to set aside time for regular reviews of progress; if this is not going according to plan, it may be necessary to change the original plans and schedules rather than try to conform to them.

Refreezing

The final stage of change is that of consolidation. Even when a change appears to have been planned and implemented successfully, problems can occur. For example, new equipment may have been effectively introduced and its operators trained in its use. Those responsible for the change, however, could pat themselves on the back too soon. Operators can too easily revert to old working practices despite the new technology unless there is ongoing monitoring once the change is in place. Not until it has become incorporated into the working culture can the change be said to have been 'refrozen'.

Refreezing, therefore, involves continuous evaluation of the success of the implementation stage. Problems or dissatisfaction may occur after implementation and these need to be identified and dealt with promptly to prevent further disruption.

Responses to change

So far, this chapter has concentrated more on the process of change than on the way people react to proposed or actual change. Yet this is an area which can cause the greatest difficulties for managers.

The extent to which individuals are likely to be resistant, indifferent or supportive towards change depends on the degree to which they perceive the change will affect them personally and their way of working. People will feel threatened by change if they think it is going to affect their pay, their status, their place of work, their chances of advancement or any other aspect of their job which is important to them. They may also be resistant to change because they have suffered a surfeit of changes at work; there comes a point when people seek some kind of stability, rationally or not, in an environment of constant change.

People almost naturally appear to resist change. It seems to be part of human nature to create norms with which people feel comfortable and, if these norms are threatened, resistance occurs. Often people feel genuinely apprehensive when they hear things are likely to change, and this apprehension increases if they lack information about what is going to happen.

Kotter and Schlesinger (1979) identified the main reasons why people resisted change as:

- Parochial self-interest.
- Misunderstanding.
- Different assessments of the situation.
- Low tolerance for change.

Parochial self-interest

Subconsciously, most people put their own welfare before that of the organization. If they perceive a change as being in the organization's interests but either not in, or, worse, actively against their own interests, they will resist it. If the change, for example is perceived to be going to result in lower pay, loss of autonomy or loss of any other factor of value to the individual, he or she is likely to oppose it. This opposition, if shared with others, may result in the growth of pressure groups to prevent the change from taking place.

Misunderstanding

If communication about a proposed change has not been adequate, people are likely to misunderstand its implications for them and their jobs. If there is a lack of trust between those responsible, or held responsible, for the change and those who are going to be affected by it, misunderstanding is linked to mistrust. Rumour and conjecture are likely to result, often leading to increased resistance.

Different assessments of the situation

Enthusiasts for change often assume that everyone shares their vision of its benefits. In fact, this is rarely true since individuals have different aspirations, values and expectations. Shared assessment of the benefits of change will only result if everyone is in possession of the same amount of relevant information about it. Even then, individuals may not share the same values. If the change is going to result in increased pay for everyone, for example, only those who value pay highly are likely to see this as a benefit; others may perceive disadvantages in loss of free time or reduced overtime which accompany the increase in pay. The danger in making these kinds of generalized assumptions is that there is likely to be open disagreement with the plans for change.

Low tolerance of change

If people have strong needs for security and stability, they are likely to resist change through apprehension that it will threaten these cornerstones of their existence. They may fear that they will find it difficult to learn new skills or work practices or that they may lose the companionship of their work colleagues through relocation or reallocation of work. They will oppose the idea of change, either openly or by making excuses for why they do not support it. Reassurance and support are essential for people with these apprehensions.

INVESTIGATE

- *Think about a change at work in which you have been involved. Did you or your colleagues experience any resistance to change? Was this resistance caused by any of the reasons above?*

Coping with reactions to change

Kotter and Schlesinger (1979) identified a number of ways by which resistance to change might be reduced, noting the advantages and disadvantages of each.

Education and communication

Educating people about the change beforehand and ensuring that ideas about change are fully communicated to everyone who is likely to be affected by it will help people to understand why the change is necessary. It is particularly effective when resistance is based on inadequate or inaccurate information and when those who are responsible for initiating the change need the support of those who oppose it. However, any adequate programme of education and communication is costly in terms of time and effort and relies on a relationship of trust between those driving and those restraining the change.

Participation and involvement

Top-down imposition of change is often unsuccessful because those designing the change have failed to take into account the knowledge and expertise of the people at whom the change is aimed. Where information from others is necessary, they need to be invited to participate in planning the change. Otherwise, they can create considerable resistance at the stage of implementation.

In general, participation and involvement of everyone who will be affected by the change leads to commitment and support for its implementation. It can, however, be an enormously time-consuming process and needs careful management. If the change needs to occur in a very short space of time, it may take too long to involve other people.

Facilitation and support

When fear and apprehension of change are the main reasons for resistance, managers need to be supportive to the problems of adjustment their staff are experiencing. They might spend time reassuring people about their apprehensions and explaining the need for change. They could also provide additional support in the form of training. All this takes time and commitment from the manager as well as patience, since fears of change may be deeply rooted and difficult to remove.

Negotiation and agreement

In some cases, opposition to change can be so powerful that incentives need to be offered if the change is to go ahead. These may take the form of individual incentives, such as promotion or a generous early retirement package, or it might involve negotiating with the union so that employees receive higher pay or other appropriate rewards in return for a change in working hours. Such negotiating tactics can prove to be expensive for the organization and a manager who resorts too easily to negotiation may be seen as a target for blackmail by other resistant groups.

Manipulation and co-option

Where, for example, an individual has considerable influence over others and, thus, power to increase resistance, managers may resort to 'co-opting' that person on to their side. This is often done by giving the person some attractive role in the design and implementation of the change so that he or she is publicly seen to be supporting it. Because it is a devious way of reducing resistance, it is also often unsuccessful and can lead to greater opposition.

Explicit and implicit coercion

As with the last method, this too is not to be recommended except as a last resort. It can involve forcing people to accept a change, riding roughshod over opposition, usually because the reasons for the change are overwhelmingly stronger than any resistance to it and, no matter what tactics are employed, the change is going to be unpopular. It requires considerable personal authority and power on the part of the person who is implementing the change as well as the ability to cope with prolonged dissatisfaction during the third stage of change.

With any change you are involved in planning and implementing, you can expect there to be a certain amount of resistance. The secret lies in identifying why and where this is most likely to occur and adopting a strategy in advance to cope with it.

Change agents

When massive change at the organizational level needs to be undertaken, it is often necessary to bring in a 'change agent'. Organizations prefer stability and, like individuals, resist change because of the upheaval it will cause. Senior management within the organization are not usually the most adept at planning radical change since they themselves have a stake in preserving the status quo. The change agent, on the other hand, may be an independent consultant or may be recruited as a full-time member of the organization's staff.

The change agent brings a fresh and generally unbiased approach to designing a programme of change. He or she works with members of the organization at all levels, identifying the problems and helping them to generate solutions. Often, the change agent will take responsibility for implementing the solutions, particularly if they are likely to be unpopular with large sections of staff.

> David Kitchen, Personnel Director of the private healthcare company BUPA, describes himself as a 'change agent'. He was recruited when BUPA had just recorded a significant loss in its medical insurance division and he was given the task of replacing half the company's board and making thousands of staff redundant at a time when both the public and private healthcare sectors were experiencing massive changes at the end of 1991.

Summary

Change is part of working life and every manager is likely to be involved in planning, managing or implementing change as part of his or her job. Pressures to change can come from outside the organization and can include social, technological, political, economic, environmental and market-related factors. They can also originate from within the organization, either from senior management who recognize the need for change or from the employees themselves.

Pressures for change can be described as the forces that drive the need for change. There are also, nearly always, opposing or restraining forces which may include financial and other resource constraints, people's reactions to proposed changes and legal or other restrictions. If these restraining forces are as strong as those driving the change, equilibrium results. In order to change the state of equilibrium, either the driving forces need to be increased or the strength of the restraining forces must be reduced.

Changes can also take place at different levels – individual, group or organizational. The level at which the change occurs will be directly related to the expected degree of difficulty you are likely to encounter in implementing it, and the length of time it will take to put it into place.

Planning and implementing change usually requires a three-stage approach consisting of unfreezing existing work practices and attitudes, changing to new practices and refreezing these as part of organizational, group and individual working culture.

There is a tendency for people to resist change owing to their own perceptions that change is likely to affect them adversely. Often, they are not fully aware of why the change is necessary and this is usually the result of poor communication between managers and their staff. A number of ways to reduce resistance to change have been suggested, including better education of, and communication with, everyone affected by it, increasing participation and involvement, providing support for natural apprehension about change and the offering of incentives. Finally, there may be a role for the 'change agent', who may be brought into an organization to effect radical change.

Activities

Think of a change at work in which you were personally involved.

1

Identify:
  (a) any external pressures for change;
  (b) any internal pressures for change.

2   At which level(s) did the change take place:
(a) individual;
(b) group;
(c) organizational?

---

3   Draw a foruefield analysis of the change, identifying the driving and restraining forces and indicating their relative strengths.

---

4   What efforts were made to:
(a) unfreeze the change;
(b) effect the change;
(c) refreeze or consolidate the change?

---

5   Was there any resistance to the idea of change or to the change itself? What were the underlying causes of this resistance?

---

6   What methods were used to reduce or overcome any resistance to change?

References

Alexander, L. D. (1985) Successfully implementing strategic decisions. *Long Range Planning*, **18**: (3)

Dawson, S. (1992) *Analysing Organisations*, 2nd edn, Macmillan, London, p. 209

Hunt, J. W. (1986) *Managing People at Work*, 2nd edn, McGraw-Hill, Maidenhead

Kotter, J. P. and Schlesinger, L. A. (1979) Choosing strategies for change. *Harvard Business Review*, March/April

Lewin, K. (1951) *Field Theory in Social Science*, Harper, London

Mayon-White, B. (ed.) (1986) *Planning and Managing Change*, Harper and Row/Open University, London

Moss Kanter, R. (1992) *The Change Masters*, Routledge, London

Further reading

Moss Kanter, R. (1992) *The Change Masters*, Routledge, London (originally published 1984, George, Allen & Unwin)

Stewart, V. (1983) *Change: The Challenge for Management*, McGraw-Hill, Maidenhead

Toffler, A. (1985) *The Adaptive Corporation*, Pan, London

Index

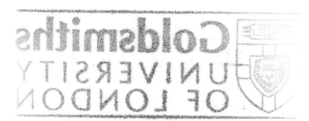

Goldsmiths
UNIVERSITY
OF LONDON

Centre
for Public and
Voluntary Sector
Development